THE FOURFOLD PILGRIMAGE

The Estates of Innocence, Misery, Grace, and Glory in Seventeenth-Century Literature

Diane Elizabeth Dreher

UNIVERSITY
PRESS OF
AMERICA

Copyright © 1982 by

University Press of America, Inc.

P.O. Box 19101, Washington, D.C. 20036

ISBN (Perfect): 0-8191-2178-9
ISBN   (Cloth): 0-8191-2177-0

Library of Congress Catalog Card Number: **81-40829**

To my teachers, who showed me the way;
my students, companions on the journey;
and my dearest friends, the blessings on
life's pilgrimage.

This book itself reflects a pilgrimage, and I acknowledge in its progress assistance from many people. To Stanley Stewart, who many years ago introduced me to seventeenth-century literature, I owe a great debt of gratitude. To my professors at UCLA, George Guffey, Paul Jorgensen, Earl Miner, and the late H.T. Swedenberg and James E. Phillips I am thankful for all that they shared with me of their knowledge of the Renaissance and seventeenth century. I would also like to thank Norma MacCaskey and Geneva Phillips for their advice on theology and metaphysics.

I acknowledge the support of UCLA in the form of a Lily Bess Campbell fellowship for research at the Huntington Library, which enabled me to do much of the background research for this book. I am grateful to the staffs of the Henry E. Huntington and William Andrews Clark Memorial Libraries for all of their assistance, and would like to thank the Huntington Library for permission to reprint the illustrations from Joseph Fletcher's The Historie of the Perfect-Cursed-Blessed Man.

I would like to thank my family, especially my grandmother Corinne Hearte, my parents Colonel Frank H. Dreher and Mary Ann Dreher, and my cousins Norma MacCaskey and Jerry Garrison. To my friends at UCLA, and my colleagues, students, and friends at the University of Santa Clara I am grateful for their continuing support and inspiration, and for sharing the journey with me in so many inexplicable ways. I am thankful to William James Stover for advice and assistance with this manuscript, to Elizabeth Moran, William Barker, George Sullwold, Judy Dunbar, Carolyn Naylor, William Sullivan, Jeff Capaccio, and many others, to Mary Jackson for typing this manuscript, and to the readers with whom I share it.

> May the peace of the Lord be always with you
> and may your pilgrimage be a happy one.

Diane Elizabeth Dreher
Santa Clara, California, 1981

The photographs of the four estates included in this study are taken from Joseph Fletcher's The Historie of the Perfect-Cursed-Blessed Man (London, 1629) and reproduced by permission of The Henry E. Huntington Library and Art Gallery, San Marino, California.

TABLE OF CONTENTS

TABLE OF CONTENTS (Continued)

Stirpe sacrâ, morsu scelerato, sanguine Divo,
Integer, infælix, & benedictus Homo.

יְהֹוָה

As in Adam all die, euen so in Christe
shall all be made aliue. 1.Co.15.22.

CHAPTER I

INTRODUCTION

The ancient precept <u>nosce teipsum</u> was followed enthusiastically in the English Renaissance and early seventeenth century. In an age suddenly aware of new worlds and a new concept of the universe, many people also sought to discover more about the microcosmic worlds of themselves. Set against the living metaphor of the Book of Nature and the theory of correspondences, their search for identity involved them personally in the complete panorama of Christian history as they recalled the infinite bliss promised them in paradise and their tragic loss of it in the Fall. A sixteenth-century translation of Calvin emphasized that "the knowledge of our selves first standeth in this point, . . . considering what was given us in creation," and contrasting this with "our miserable estate after the fall of Adam."[1] Because Calvin and his followers saw human life as both individual and allegorical, their search for self-knowledge gave a new emblematic significance to their lives, revealing divine truths and repeating biblical history before their eyes.

By the seventeenth century this allegorical view of existence had developed into an ideological framework as pervasive and influential as the Great Chain of Being. As he progressed through life from childhood to maturity, an individual of this period was believed to pass through the four spiritual "estates" of Innocence, Misery, Grace, and Glory, which paralleled the four stages of Christian history: Eden, the Fall, the Redemption, and the Last Judgment. Each redeemed Christian thus recapitulated the history of his race, falling from the relative innocence of childhood into the State of sin and Misery, where he remained until a dramatic "conversion experience" reenacted the Redemption on a personal level, bringing him into the State of Grace. Then, assured of his election, he looked forward to the State of Glory in the afterlife. In the following study, I will trace the history and development of this concept, which dominated the works of many of the major writers of the period.

The four estates can be traced back to Augustine's <u>Enchiridion,</u> written in the late fourth century. "Of the . . . four different stages of man," Augustine declared, "the first is before the law, the second is under the law, the third is under grace, and the fourth is in full and perfect peace." However, Augustine maintained that the first estate for the individual was not edenic innocence, but ignorance, appetite, and original sin, from which one falls into a more serious state of sin. As he explained:

1

When, in the deepest shadows of ignorance, he lives
according to the flesh with no restraint of reason--this
is the primal state of man. Afterward, when "through
the law the knowledge of sin" has come to man, and
the Holy Spirit has not yet come to his aid--so that even
if he wishes to live according to the law, he is vanquished--
man sins knowingly and is brought under the spell and
made the slave of sin," for by whatever a man is van-
quished, of this master he is the slave." The effect of
the knowledge of the law is that sin works in man the
whole round of concupiscence, which adds to the guilt
of the first transgression. And thus it is that what was
written is fulfilled: "The law entereth in, that the offense might abound." This is the second state of man.

But if God regards a man with solicitude so that he
then believes in God's help in fulfilling His commands,
and if a man begins to be led by the Spirit of God, then
the mightier power of love struggles against the power
of the flesh. And although there is still in man a power
that fights against him--his infirmity being not yet fully
healed--yet he lives by faith and lives righteously in so
far as he does not yield to evil desires, conquering them
by his love of righteousness. This is the third state of
the man of good hope.

A final peace is in store for him who continues to go
forward in this course toward perfection through stead-
fast piety. This will be perfected beyond this life in the
repose of the spirit, and, at the last, in the resurrection
of the body.[2]

Augustine saw this evolution within the individual paralleled by
four stages in Christian history. In the Enchiridion he explained that,
"Thus, also, the history of God's people had been ordered by successive
temporal epochs, as it pleased God, who 'ordered all things in measure
and number and weight.' The first period was before the law; the second
under the law, which was given through Moses; the next, under grace
which was revealed through the first Advent of the Mediator." The
fourth estate, as he described it in a later passage, was to be the Glory
of the Second Coming and the Last Judgment.[3]

In his spiritual autobiography, the Confessions, Augustine described
his own progression through these estates. He explained how the corruptions of his childhood had led him to a second, more serious state of sin,
refuting the Pelagian convictions about the innocence of childhood with
personal experience. "I pilfered from my parents' cellar and table, sometimes driven by gluttony, sometimes just to have something to give to
other boys in exchange for their baubles," he related, noting that "these
same sins as we grow older are transferred from tutors and masters; they
pass from nuts and balls and sparrows, to magistrates and kings, to gold

2

and lands and slaves, just as the rod is succeeded by more severe chas-
tisements."[4] Condemning his later fall into carnal pleasures, he explained
how "as the mists of passion steamed out of the puddly concupiscence of
the flesh, and the hot imagination of puberty,"[5] he "fell among men, de-
lerious in their pride, carnal and voluble, whose mouths were the snares
of the devil."[6]

Then at length Augustine described his dramatic conversion experience. As he reflected on his sins, "there arose a mighty storm [within
him], accompanied by a mighty rain of tears . . . . I flung myself down
underneath a fig tree--how I know not--and gave free course to my tears."
Weeping and asking himself how much longer he was to continue in this
sinful state, he suddenly heard the voice of a child chanting "Pick it up,
read it." He opened his Bible and read, "put on the Lord Jesus Christ,
and make no provision for the flesh,"[7] and from that moment he was a
changed man. For the remainder of the Confessions he celebrated the
grace of God which led him to his conversion, and looked to the glory of
the world to come.

Following the example of Augustine's Confessions, the sermons,
devotional manuals and spiritual autobiographies of the sixteenth and seventeenth centuries resounded with the theme of man's spiritual pilgrimage
through the four estates. As G.A. Starr has observed, "the belief that
spiritual life varies little from man to man . . . enabled every man to
measure his own spiritual state by that of others." Taking his cue from
other men's spiritual histories, an individual of the mid-seventeenth century believed that he would pass through four distinct stages on the way
to salvation.[8]

These stages appeared in early accounts as merely four periods in
the history of Christian mankind, with few analogies drawn to individual
experience. Godfrey Goodman's The Fall of Man (1616) described the four
estates in such terms: "in this great world you may observe, that first
there was a state of nature, which was the forerunner to the Law: then
followed the Law, which was a preparative to the Gospell: now at length
succeeds the Gospell, where in there is the fulnesse of knowledge, as
much as is befitting our nature and present condition . . . and yet we
may expect some further revelation of the mysteries of Christ's kingdome,
when wee our selves shall be more capable thereof, which shall be the
state of happinesse and glorie.[9] In his Divine Herball (also 1616), Thomas
Adams elaborated on this historical pattern, maintaining:

> Man is to be considered in a foure-fold estate. Confectionis,
> Infectionis, Refectionis, Perfectionis. First, God made
> him happy, without misery, without iniquity. . . . Heere
> is mans first draught of Gods bountie; his original state.
> 2. Then man fell from holinesse, and so from happinesse;
> and lost the favour of the Creator, with the good of the
> creature that a generall curse fell on the earth for his
> sake. . . . 3. A Redeemer is come; what is man the better
> for it, that hath no power to beleeve on him? Faith he

3

hath none, but what God must put into him. . . . Lastly
the Lord gives us Faith; and so we shall <u>receive</u> a happines by this beleeved saviour, better than ever our first
creation gave us: a kingdome; a kingdome of life; that
can never be taken from us.[10]

A year later in <u>An Exposition upon the Epistle to the Colossians</u>, Nicholas
Byfield explained the four estates in greater detail, urging men to see
them as evidence of God's mercy:

>The providence of God over man, may be considered ac-
>cording to his fourefold estate: 1. of <u>Innocencie</u>. 2. of
><u>Corruption</u>. 3. of <u>Grace</u>. 4. of <u>Glorie</u>.
>
>In the estate of <u>Innocencie</u>, faith chiefly beholds and
>wonders at the glorious <u>Image of God</u>, in which man was
>created . . . .
>
>In the state of <u>Corruption</u>, two things do offer them-
>selves to our dolefull contemplation: 1. <u>sinne</u>. 2. the
><u>punishment of sin</u>. <u>Sinne</u> is both originall and actuall . . .
>
>In the state of <u>Grace</u>, faith views three things:
>1. the <u>meanes of grace</u>. 2. the <u>subject</u>. 3. the <u>degrees</u>.
>The meanes is either <u>before time</u>, or <u>in time</u>; before
>time; tis the election of God; . . . in time, the means
>chiefly is <u>Christ</u>, and the covenant in him. . . .
>
>The fourth and last estate of man, is the <u>estate of</u>
><u>glorie</u>; which stands of three degrees. 1. <u>resurrection</u>.
>2. <u>the last judgement</u> and 3. <u>life eternall</u>.[11]

Drawing an analogy between the historical estates and individual experience, Samuel Crooke affirmed in <u>The Guide unto True Blessednesse</u>
(1625), "there is a fourefold life of man. The life of nature, the life of
corruption, the life of grace, and the life of glory. The first life <u>Adam</u>
lived before his fall. The last, the blessed live in heaven. The third, the
godly live after their conversion on earth and the second is the life of all
the unregenerate."[12]

Within the next few years more and more religious writers began
to see the four estates on these two different levels. As Thomas Wilson
emphasized in his <u>Commentary on the . . . Epistle of S. Paul to the</u>
<u>Romanes</u> (1627), there is "a threefold estate of Gods children: the first is
of corruption (they were enemies.) The second is of grace: they are jus-
tified and reconciled. The third is of glory: they shall bee saved," adding
"There is a fourth not named heere, to wit; the state of innocency by
creation." Furthermore, he insisted, "Every true Child of God must passe
through all these."[13] Every redeemed man must recapitulate the four estates in his own experience. Similarly, John Bartlet attempted to bring
men to conversion by encouraging them "to meditate on the Four-fold

4

Estate of Man, his blessed state by Creation, cursed state by Transgression, gracious state by Regeneration, and happy estate by Glorification,"[14] and Thomas Jackson discussed the estates throughout his works, convinced that they were "Estates or Conditions of Men not only in General, but of every man in particular, which finally attains unto Salvation."[15]

By the end of the first quarter of the seventeenth century, the four estates had become for many an integral part of their total world view. William Austin, for example, saw the estates as evidence of divine order on the natural as well as the historical and personal levels. This is apparent in his discussion of the four seasons of the year:

> These foure Quarters, we may compare to the foure Times of Man. The Incarnation of our Saviour, to the first Time of Mans Incarnation; (in Innocencie, in Paradise). The forerunning of John; to the Time of the Preaching of Noah, and the Patriarchs (before the Law: the Feast of Saint Michael; to the Time of the Law, (which was given, by the Ministerie of Angels): And the Feast of the Birth of our Saviour; to the Time, under the Gospel.

> Or they may be compared, to the foure Estates of every particular, and private Man. The first, of the Incarnation; to the time a Man lives in the Flesh, and in the lusts thereof (as a Naturall man). The Second, of Saint John; (who was a voice in the Wildernesse); to the time of Mans Repentance (by the preaching of the Gospel) till his death. The third; of Saint Michael: to the time of Mans Resurrection, (which shall be in Voce Archangeli). And the fourth, of our Saviour; to the Life Everlasting in Jesus Christ; which shall conclude our yeeres, for ever: and destroy all time, that there shall be no more.[16]

The literary significance of this concept was to increase even further during the next half century, as it appeared in the works of most of the major religious writers of the period, including Donne, Herbert, Vaughan, Bunyan, Traherne, and Milton. But in order to comprehend the four estates more completely, let us first examine them individually, exploring both their historical and personal implications.

NOTES

[1] John Calvin, The Institution of Christian Religion, written in Latine by M. John Calvine, and translated into English according to the Authors Last Edition, by Thomas Norton (London, 1582), pp. 70-71.

[2] Enchiridion, in Confessions and Enchiridion, trans. Albert C. Outler (London: SCM Press, 1955), pp. 409-10 (underscores mine).

[3] _Enchiridion_, p. 410.

[4] _Confessions_, in _Confessions and Enchiridion_, pp. 48-49.

[5] _Confessions_, p. 50.

[6] _Confessions_, p. 66.

[7] _Confessions_, pp. 175-76.

[8] _Defoe and Spiritual Autobiography_ (Princeton: Princeton Univ. Press, 1965), pp. 17-18.

[9] _The Fall of Man or the Corruption of Nature_ (London, 1616), p. 5 (underscores mine).

[10] _A Divine Herball Together with a Forrest of Thornes. In Five Sermons_ (London, 1616), p. 93.

[11] _An Exposition upon the Epistle to the Colossians_ (London, 1617), Epistle Dedicatory, sig. ¶2v.

[12] _The Guide Unto True Blessednesse, or a Body of the Doctrine of the Scriptures directing man to the saving knowledge of God_ (London, 1625), p. 51.

[13] _A Commentary on the Most Divine Epistle of S. Paul to the Romanes_ (London, 1627), p. 153.

[14] _The Practical Christian_ (London, 1670), p. 133.

[15] _A Treatise of the Primaeval Estate of the First Man_, in _The Works of the Reverend and Learned Divine, Thomas Jackson, D.D._ (London, 1673), III, 156.

[16] _In Festo Sancti Michaelis Archangeli: An Essay of Tutular Angels_ (London, 1635), p. 254.

The State of Innocence

CHAPTER II

THE STATE OF INNOCENCE

The Historical Concept

The concept of the State of Innocence, in its countless manifestations, expresses perhaps the most basic of human longings. Anthropologists claim that the image of a lost paradise and its accompanying nostalgia are universal human phenomena.[1] An archetypal motif in art and mythology, this vision of perfection has taken many forms. For the ancient Greeks it was the Golden Age, described by Hesiod in his Works and Days, as the "golden race of mortal men" during the time of Chronos who lived "like gods without sorrow of heart, remote and free from toil and grief: miserable age rested not on them; but with legs and arms never failing they made merry with feasting beyond the reach of all evils . . . and they had all good things: for the fruitful earth unforced bare them fruit abundantly and without stint. They dwelt in ease and peace upon their lands with many good things, rich in flocks and loved by the blessed gods."[2] Free from the ravages of time and toil, this life of joy and abundance beckoned to people in the Renaissance as they saw themselves, like their Greek counterparts, confined by the demands of a degenerate Age of Iron.

For Theocritus, Virgil, and their Renaissance successors, the dream of Eden flourished in the pastoral tradition, which reflected our everpresent desire for a retreat from the corruptions and complexities of civilization to the simpler harmony of nature.[3] A traditional vehicle for social criticism, the pastoral in its contrived simplicity embodies a society's ideals, drawing by implication a sharp contrast with its more corrupt realities. In the literature of the English Renaissance, the pastoral was used by Skelton, Wyatt, Spenser, Sidney, Shakespeare, Jonson, and Herrick, to name only a few. The many variations on this tradition in the Renaissance, from Arcadia to the Forest of Arden attest to the popularity of the pastoral and the idea that perfection could be approached more easily by returning to nature and our most primitive state than by employing all the arts of civilization.

The exploration and travel accounts of the Renaissance mark an important change in perceptions of the State of Innocence. As Henri Baudet has explained, whereas our culture had formerly conceived of Eden "in terms of time, seeking it in our own or in another 'absolute' past," in the Renaissance people began to seek it "in terms of space," in their own world.[4] Primitivism, with its glorification of the "noble savage" was a direct outgrowth of the pastoral tradition, which had always associated perfection with a primitive culture. When they found that such cultures still existed, so great was their desire for the state of lost innocence that Renaissance explorers sought it on distant shores. New worlds drew them on with an irresistible power, seeming to promise fulfillment of all of their dreams of paradise. Proximity and familiarity invariably disclosed the flaws, but their first glimpse at an unknown territory, a "new" land, gleaming in its expansive greenness undoubtedly made them feel that they had escaped from the confines of Renaissance civilization (all too full of sin and human error) to the dizzy realm of dreams where anything was possible. The Indians--tall, graceful, nearly naked, and apparently without shame or sense of sin--reminded them of Adam and Eve before the Fall and offered an intriguing alternative to their established way of life, leading ultimately to the primitivism of Rousseau and the revolutions and social reforms of a later age.

The Renaissance fascination with the historical garden of Eden is evident in the numerous accounts written on the Creation and the Fall. Many writers of the period also referred in their descriptions to the classical Golden Age, considering it merely the pagan apprehension of the State of Innocence. In his description of Eden, for example, Dante stated that "they who in olden times sang of the golden age and its happy state, perchance dreamed in Parnassus of this place."[5] Similarly, Sir Walter Ralegh declared in his History of the World (1614), "Besides, whence had Homer his invention of Alcinous gardens, as Justin Martyr noteth, but out of Moses his description of Paradise? . . . and whence are their praises of Elysian fieldes, but out of the Storie of Paradise? to which also appertaine those verses of the golden age in Ovid."[6] And Godfrey Goodman concluded, "When Poets so often mention the golden age, what doe they else, but point out the state of man's first happinesse, integritie, and innocencie."[7] Thus, drawing upon classical as well as Christian backgrounds, Renaissance descriptions of Eden luxuriated in the depiction of the ideal. Let us turn to some of these descriptions to see more clearly how this first estate must have appeared to the Renaissance mind.

The garden of Eden described in Genesis 2:8-14 was a lush and fertile paradise, abounding in beauty and delight. With its fruitful trees, precious gems, and exotic rivers, the biblical description is sensuous enough to begin with, but even more so are the many accounts of paradise written in the Renaissance, when it was commonly believed that Eden could still be found somewhere in the Eastern world. As a modern scholar has observed, "the Renaissance flourished with maps and treatises describing its position, now east, now west, now on an island, now behind or upon a mountain--but always remote, always inaccessible." Christopher Columbus thought he had found it across the sea and Samuel Purchas and Peter Heylyn were among the many who speculated on its location.[8] Isidore of Seville believed that paradise was on a mountaintop near the moon, separated from the rest of the world by a broad expanse of ocean,[9] while the Manichees thought paradise had once encompassed the entire earth. Tertullian, Bonaventure, and Durandas believed it was located

10

under the equinoctial pole, and Postellus thought it was under the North Pole.[10] Sir Walter Ralegh, providing a map to back up his argument, declared positively that

> Paradise was a place created by God, and a part of this
> our earth and habitable world, seated in the lower part of
> the Region of Eden, afterward called Aram fluviorum, or
> Mesopotamia, which taketh into it also a portion of Shinar
> and Armenia: this Region standing in the most excellent
> temper of all other, (to wit) 35 degrees from the Aequinoc-
> tiall and 55 from the North pole: in which Climate the
> most excellent wines, fruites, oyle, graine of all sorts are
> to this day found in abundance. And there is nothing that
> better proveth the excellence of this sayd soile and tem-
> per, then the abundant growing of the Palm-trees, without
> the care and labour of man. For wherein soever the
> Earth, Nature, and the Sunne can most vaunt, that they
> have excelled, yet shall this Plant be the greatest wonder
> of all their works: this tree alone giveth unto man what-
> soever his life beggeth at Nature's hand.[11]

Ralegh's commentary on the location of paradise may have been disputed by his contemporaries,[12] but his belief in the garden of Eden as an actual place in the physical world and his description of its natural abundance were Renaissance commonplaces. As this translation of St. Isidore reveals, paradise was synonymous with delight:

> Paradyse is a place situated in the Orientall parts of the
> world, whose aetimology (the word being translated out
> of the Greeks into Latin) signifieth hortum, a Garden.
> In Hebrew it is called Heden, which interpreted in Latin
> is the same that deliciae, delights: wherefore both names
> being joyned together, they signifie a Garden of all man-
> ner of delights, and pleasures, a place beset with all kinde
> of fruitfull, and beautiful trees: where there is neyther
> cold, nor heat, but a perpetual temper of aire; furthermore
> out of this so pleasant a place there floweth in great
> aboundance, a faire fountaine which watereth the whole
> Garden and trees thereof.[13]

To St. Basil, as well, paradise was blessed with harmony, abundance, and celestial radiance:

> a place flowing with all sorts of pleasure and delights,
> surpassing farre the beauty of all sensible creatures,
> which by reason of the height it hath, admitteth no
> obscurity of night, or darknesse by clouds, but rather
> is alwaies resplendent with the shining of the orientall
> starres: to which place also there can come no immod-
> erate force of windes, no storme, no tempest, no horrour
> of winter, no inundation by waters, no burning of Sommer,

11

no drought of Autumne, but a continuall and peacable tem-
perature of all times and all seasons, insomuch that, that
which may bee justly thought the best and most pleasant of
every severall time of the yeare, that doth alwaies heere
concur and abound, to wit, a continuall pleasure of the spring,
the aboundance of harvest, the mirth and alacrity of Autumne,
with the rest and quietnesse of the winter.[14]

In his account, written in 1596, Gervase Babington agreed that paradise
was created for human delight, for "God set in this Paradise, things not
onely profitable for use, but pleasant also for sight, thereby assuring us,
that he disliketh not our pleasures anymore then our necessaries, but most
gratiously aloweth, that wee should have both."[15] In Eden, then, according
to these accounts, Adam and Eve were surrounded by beauty and abundance. They existed in a state of perfect harmony in a fruitful land that
required no cultivation, no arduous labor,[16] with a temperate climate that
knew no change of seasons, no extremes. With all of their needs ostensi-
bly satisfied by the benevolent torpor of their environment, they were
committed to a life of peace and idyllic pleasure.

Created in the image of God and thus embodying the goodness and
harmony of their creator, they had only to enjoy the paradise they had
been given, to rule benignly over all the other creatures, as the Bible
states in Genesis 1:27-28. John Salkeld explained in A Treatise of Paradise (1617) that man in "his happie estate of innocencie" was created
"good in substance, in nature excellent, in his powers perfect."[17] To
Thomas Wilson, author of A Christian Dictionary (1630), the most out-
standing thing about Adam and Eve in this first estate was their radiant
perfection, their "voydnesse of fault, and freedome from al sinne."[18] For
man and woman were created in God's image and in Eden that image
shone forth with all of its prelapsarian splendor.

According to Nicholas Byfield and others, this image of God consisted of the three principal virtues of "Knowledge, Holynesse, and Righteousnesse."[19] Samuel Crooke, however, treated this matter in greater
detail. Adam and Eve, he believed, reflected God's image in:

> foure singular excellencies: viz.
>
> 1. A reasonable and immortal soule.
>
> 2. True wisdome and holinesse, adorning the Soule, wherein
> especially he resembled his Maker.
>
> 3. A body endued with beautie, strength, and immortalitie,
> answerable to the soule.
>
> 4. Dominion over the creatures.
>
> [With] the Image of God, in wisdome and true holinesse,
> shining in him without teinture or blemish, hee enjoyed

12

full fruition and assurance of the favourable and blissefull presence of his Creator, together with absolute contentment in himselfe, and service from all the creatures, to whom as their Lord, hee gave their original names.[20]

According to other commentators, however, the image of God rested primarily in our "understanding mind which is . . . , such as is not in other creatures."[21] The image of God, for them, signified the image of the Trinity figured in the human mind, which consisted of the three-fold powers of memory, will, and understanding. This theory was held by Sir Thomas Browne, Thomas Heywood, and John Davies of Hereford, among others.[22] Ralegh supported it in his History, maintaining that "as in the Minde there are three distinct powers, or faculties (to wit) Memorie, Understanding, and Will, and yet all these are three distinct persons, the Father, Sonne, and Holy Ghost, and yet but one God."[23] Joseph Fletcher described this theory poetically, explaining that

> This Soule, like Gods Essentialitie
> Containeth in't a threefold facultie,
> Whereby the Trinity is figured,
> That God-like Man maight be more honoured.
> First is the Minde, which giveth pow'r and skill,
> Wherby we know, we judge what's good, what's ill.
> Next is the Will, begotten of the Minde;
> For till we know, to will we'r not enclinde.
> Then from the Mindes conceipt, and Wills affection
> Proceeds an active Pow'r of Operation.[24]

Thomas Traherne, in Meditations on the Six Days of the Creation, also praised this harmony within the human soul asking his readers to "Consider, in the Soul of Man, the divine Image, by these three Faculties, Understanding, Will, and Memory, which in the Soul are one, having thus an Impress of the Trinity within it."[25]

Man in the State of Innocence was the image of God, then, in body, mind, and soul and in his sovereignty over all creation. All of his faculties were in perfect harmony and one with divine will. As Thomas Aquinas stated in the Summa Theologica, "man was so appointed in the state of innocence, that there was no rebellion of the flesh against the spirit."[26] Temperance in Edèn was not a concerted effort, but a state of being. Free from the ravages of excessive passions and internal turmoil, Adam and Eve experienced a natural serenity and peace of mind that was paradise in itself.

Many people in the Renaissance contemplated this aspect of the State of Innocence with a mixture of wonder and regret. Only too aware of the passionate internal struggles of postlapsarian mankind, John Donne reflected in one of his sermons that "in the state of innocency" man's "affections submitted themselves to reason, so that he had no inward enemy."[27] How incredible this must have seemed to the author of the agonized Holy Sonnets.

13

Hermeticist Thomas Vaughan offered a more elaborate description of Adam's psychological state:

> Man in the beginning (I mean the substantiall inward man) both in, and after his Creation for some short time was a pure intellectual Essence, free from all fleshly, sensuall Affections. In this state the Anima, or sensitive Nature did not prevail over the spiritual, as it does now in us. For the superior Mentall part of Man was united to God per Contactum Essentialem, and the Divine Light being received in and conveyed to the inferior portions of the Soul did mortifie all carnall desires, insomuch that in Adam the sensitive Faculties were scarce at all imployed, the spirituall prevailing over them in him, as they do over the Spirituall now in us.[28]

For Vaughan, Adam in the State of Innocence experienced not merely a harmonious balance of reason and passion, but divine reason actually overpowered his carnal desires, making of him "a pure intellectual Essence." Vaughan's view of Eden, in which man's "sensitive Faculties were scarce at all imployed," differs considerably from Milton's description in Paradise Lost, in which Eden is a lush, fragrant, and frankly sensuous paradise. The extent of human sensuality before the Fall remained a question for debate throughout the Renaissance. However, the church fathers and Renaissance theologians did agree that the prelapsarian individual perceived his or her world harmoniously, with none of the crises and conflicts of motivation that beset modern mankind.

In addition to harmonious minds, our prelapsarian ancestors had harmonious bodies, created in perfect beauty and health. As Edmund Bonner stated in A Profitable and Necessarie Doctrine, "The body of man, in the estate of originall innocencie, had in it helth, strength, cumlines, and other like qualities, in the highest degre of perfection."[29] And John Bartlet added, man "was made the most excellent of all the sensible creatures, as appears, . . . In respect of the structure of his Body, and the endowments of his Soul."[30] In body as in soul, then, they reflected the glory of their creator.

All weakness, all disease and pain were unknown in Eden. Adam and Eve perceived their bodies only as the expression of their will, as one with their minds and souls. Incapacity, fear, and self-doubt were foreign to them. Resplendent in their native innocence and grace, they walked through paradise, in harmony with themselves, one another, and all creation. Milton described them in Paradise Lost as two noble beings, "Godlike erect, with native Honour clad" who "In naked Majestie seemd Lords of all," (IV, 289-90).[31] Not only did they shine with "The image of thir glorious Maker" (IV, 292); for Milton they were also archetypes for masculine and feminine beauty. Adam was strong, heroic, like a Greek God; Eve soft, alluring, submissive:

14

His fair large Front and Eye sublime declar'd
Absolute rule; and Hyacinthin Locks
Round from his parted forelock manly hung
Clustring, but not beneath his shoulders broad:
Shee as a vail down to the slender waste
Her unadorned golden tresses wore
Dissheveld; but in wanton ringlets wav'd
As the Vine curles her tendrils, which impli'd
Subjection, but requir'd with gentle sway
And by her yielded, by him best receiv'd.

                                        (IV, 300-09)

Adam's intellectual powers were also a matter of much discussion.
Thomas Aquinas, among others, believed that Adam's perception was much
greater than that of fallen man, who sees "through a glass darkly." "Man
in the state of innocence," according to Aquinas, "saw God immediately.
. . . He also saw without an enigma," without obscurity, for "obscurity
resulted from sin." Aquinas claimed that Adam's knowledge was "mid-way
between our knowledge in the present state and the knowledge we shall
have in heaven."[32] While most commentators mentioned Adam's knowledge of astronomy and natural history, Thomas Jackson praised his memory as well,[33] and John Salkeld held that Adam, like Solomon, possessed
great wisdom, the ability "to know how the world was made, and the op-
eration of the elements: the beginning, ending, and midst of the times:
the alterations of the turning of the Sunne, and the change of seasons:
the circuits of yeeres, and the positions of the starres: the natures of
living creatures, and the furies of wilde beasts: the violence of windes,
and the reasoning of men: the diversities of plants, and the vertues of
roots: and all such things, as are either secret, or manifest."[34]

However, some of the commentators were not so convinced of
Adam's supreme wisdom. Denied the information available from experience, Adam's knowledge, they argued, was extremely limited. Rivetus,
for example, claimed that Adam had been given only enough knowledge
to recognize God as his creator, to live wisely and prudently, and to gov-
ern the other creatures.[35] Of other things not directly related to his state
he was ignorant. To Theophilus, Adam's knowledge was limited not only
by his lack of experience, but by his immaturity. He maintained that
"Adam before the Fall was in age still an infant, wherefore he was not
able to receive knowledge worthily."[36]

According to many commentators, then, Adam and Eve in the State
of Innocence were paradoxically equipped with a keener mind but less
knowledge than their postlapsarian descendents. Their actions were not
based upon the reasoned choice between good and evil that Milton described in Areopagitica, but instead upon an intuitive awareness of good.
As John Woolton stated in A Newe Anatomie of whole man (1576), "Before the Fall of our Parentes, when nature was innocent & uncorrupted,
this light of wisdome, and intelligence of things divine and humaine, did
shyne brightly in man: neither had he then only sparks & sedes, but a

15

plentiful storehouse & flowing fountaine of all vertue."[37] Adam's intuition, which Woolton believed could be better understood by comparing it to the instincts of animals, made him "a sufficient lawe and scholemaster to himself."[38]

Spared the dynamic opposition of good and evil in their world and in themselves, Adam and Eve led a simple existence and functioned like obedient, trusting children. Consequently, they knew an inner peace impossible to people in this fallen world. As Christopher Lever emphasized in The Holy Pilgrim (1609), "Adam in the state of his innocence, had this condition of happinesse . . . he was in ful favor of God, a joy unexpressable."[39] Completely integrated in the harmony of the universe, Adam knew no separation, no doubt, no fear. Like a child sheltered by his loving parents, Adam was surrounded by the radiance of divine grace. As Bartlet explained, God was present within him; "he was made the Habitation, and Temple of the Holy Ghost."[40] Paradise, John Downame agreed, was a state of harmony and "securitie . . . a perfect tranquillitie of the minde without the encounters of any feares, which was wrought in our first Parents by the Lord our Creator, and was a fruit of their full assurance of God's protection and providence continually watching over them, wherby they were assured of freedome from all evill, . . . and that outward peace which they had with all the visible Creatures, none of which could hurt them, all of which were usefull and serviceable unto them."[41]

Descriptions of such a paradise, a life idyllic in its native simplicity, led many men and women of the Renaissance to disparage civilization and sing the praises of primitivism. Eden was a romantic ideal long before the onset of nineteenth century Romanticism. As Arnold Williams has observed, the State of Innocence was traditionally associated with "the simple godly life." In Eden "luxury had not yet made its appearance. No superfluous clothes adorned Adam and Eve, who were content with their own naked modesty. The evils that followed the introduction of riches were yet unknown."[42] The ideals of paradise, the temperance of Adam and Eve, and their freedom from riches and private property were admired and emulated in varying degrees by the utopian societies and religious reform movements of the mid-seventeenth century. Henry Vaughan's translation of Boethius reflects this desire for reform:

> Happy that first white age! when wee
> Lived by the Earths meere Charitie,
> No soft luxurious Diet then
> Had effeminated men,
> No other meat, nor wine had any
> Then the Course Mast, or simple honey,
> And by the Parents care layd up
> Cheap Berries did the Children sup.
> No pompous weare was in those dayes
> Of gummie Silks, or Skarlet bayes,
> Their beds were on some flowrie brink
> And clear Spring-water was their drink.

16

The shadie Pine in the Suns heat
Was their Coole and known Retreat.[43]

The nostalgia for the simple things and basic suspicion of civilization we find in Vaughan recurs in a great number of the accounts of the State of Innocence written during this period.

But even in Eden there were obligations; as we learn from Genesis 2:15-17, Adam and Eve were required to "dresse" and "keepe" the garden, and to refrain from eating the forbidden fruit. Although, as Godfrey Goodman stated, "men lived free from the sweate of their browes" in Eden,[44] they did not live there in idleness. For Milton, who stressed the "service" of men and angels in Paradise Lost and other religious writers as well, idleness had no part in the divine plan. Gervase Babington explained that "God set man in this Garden, to dresse and keepe it, not allowing Men in his most innocencie to bee idle: no, hee would not his Angels to want what to doe, but made them ministring spirits."[45] The commentators agreed that labor existed before the Fall, but not hard, arduous toil. The latter was the effect of the curse on Adam after the Fall, the former an act of service toward God.

The major requirement of the "Covenant of Works, which God made with Adam in the state of Innocency"[46] was, of course, to abstain from eating the forbidden fruit. The necessity of law, of limits, even in Eden, was discussed by many commentators, who saw man's nobility in the exercise of his free will. John Diodati commended this "law, even in the state of innocency, by which man might also know by experience, his true happinesse, if he persisted in innocency; or his unhappiness, if he disobeyed this commandement of tryall."[47] As we shall see in a later chapter, this one prohibition was, for Milton, a necessary exercise of human reason, the one faculty which set us above the animals. In Areopagitica (1644), he held that "when God gave [man] reason, he gave him freedom to choose, for reason is but choosing; he had bin else a meer artificial Adam, such an Adam as he is in the motions."[48]

Before its destruction by the knowledge of good and evil, the harmony of the State of Innocence was unbroken by an awareness of time. Blessed with a temperate climate, as we have seen, Eden knew no change of season, no contrasting extremes of heat and cold. Likewise, Adam and Eve, created in their prime, would never have known the effects of aging, had they not fallen. In fact, Henry More believed that "the State of Innocence was to have been eternal,"[49] that Adam and Eve were merely to persevere in goodness and innocence forever.

However, other theologians, unable to accept such an unchanging state, postulated that if Adam and Eve had proven themselves, they would ultimately have been taken up to heaven. In Eden, according to Godfrey Goodman, "there should have been no death . . . but some happie translation."[50] And John Diodati, also aware of the need for change and progression in human life, stated that man, after a "most happy, contented, equal and immortal life . . . should have been without old age, paines,

17

sicknesses, drooping, or death, transported into the celestial and eternall
. . . if he persevered in his obedience to God."[51] Milton, as well, declared
that by "true love" and devotion Adam and Eve might have ascended to a
state of "heav'nly love" (VIII, 586-91).

But whether or not they believed in an eventual "translation," all
the commentators conceived of Eden as a state beyond time, a continuous
flow of goodness and beauty. In The Enclosed Garden, Stanley Stewart
points out the paradoxical nature of this ideal, which "contradicts the
hardest fact of human life. Yet," he emphasizes, "no idea is more firmly
rooted in Christian thought than that of experience not bound by time."[52]
Life in such a timeless paradise, in which all of our needs are anticipated
by a benevolent deity, where there is no evil, no duplicity, no pain, no
dangerous work, no suspense, seems on the surface to be everything all
humans dream of. Like the lovers forever suspended in time in Keats's
"Ode on a Grecian Urn," this vision of edenic perfection appeals to our
everpresent desire to escape from a world of limits, disappointment, and
change.

Innocence and the Individual

To many people in the Renaissance, Eden existed not only in the
macrocosm but also in the microcosm or the inner world of man's mind.
This interpretation can be traced back in part to the church fathers, including Origen, who saw in the Old Testament description of paradise an
allegorical representation of the human soul,[53] and St. Ambrose, who
stated: "Paradise is, therefore, a land of fertility--that is to say, a soul
which is fertile--planted in Eden, that is, in a certain delightful or well-
tilled land in which the soul finds pleasure."[54] In the early seventeenth
century, Ralegh referred to these theologians, who "by the place or garden of Paradise, . . . meant the soule or minde."[55]

In this period the State of Innocence was progressively associated
with the soul in childhood, as the child in his or her relative innocence
was believed to recapitulate the unfallen state of Adam and Eve. The
allegorical parallels are obvious. The child is, in many ways, a true primitive, completely ignorant and thus unspoiled by civilization.[56] Provided
by their parents with all the necessities, they are temporarily protected
from the evils of the world around them. Free, for the most part, from
burdensome toil and sheltered by a loving family, children in their youthful innocence are set apart from the race of fallen mankind.

In the atmosphere of reevaluation encouraged by the new science,
the child was seen as intrinsically different from adults. As Philip Aries
has observed, this difference was reflected in children's clothing. In the
Middle Ages a child "was dressed just like the other men and women of
his class. . . . Nothing in medieval dress distinguished the child from the
adult." Seemingly unaware of the different proportions of the human
body in childhood and adulthood, medieval painters portrayed children as
strange, doll-like miniatures, standing at the feet of adults. However,

18

with the humanistic emphasis in art and the study of human anatomy, artists became more aware of the human body and children began to look like children. In addition, as Aries notes, "In the seventeenth century . . . the child, or at least the child of quality, whether noble or middle class, ceased to be dressed like the grown-up. . . . henceforth he had an outfit reserved for his age group, which set him apart from the adults. This can be seen from the first glimpse at any of the numerous child portraits painted at the beginning of the seventeenth century."[57]

Simultaneous with this new apprehension of childhood was the association of childhood with innocence, a concept drawn from many sources. Iconographically, early Renaissance painters began to represent angels as children instead of adults, perhaps "because they thought of little children as more symbolic of angelic purity."[58] The association of childhood with innocence was reinforced by the metaphysical lore of alchemy. According to the alchemists, gold was the symbol of the original and uncorrupted state of the soul.[59] This theory was set forth in John Everard's translation of the Divine Pymander (1650), in which Hermes states:

> Consider, O Son, the Soul of a Childe, when as yet
> it hath received no dissolution of its Body, which is not
> grown, but is very small: how then if it look upon it
> self, it sees it self beautiful, as not having been yet
> spotted with the Passions of the Body, but as it were
> depending yet upon the Soul of the World.

> But when the Body is grown and distracteth, the
> Soul it ingenders Forgetfulness, and partakes no more
> of the Fair, and the Good, and Forgetfulness is Evilness.[60]

In addition, as Louis Martz has noted, the poems of Henry Vaughan reflect his belief in the memory of a "beata vita" or platonic pre-existence still alive in the mind of the child.[61] In poems like "The Retreate" Vaughan looked back nostalgically to this early experience of harmony:

> Happy those early dayes! when I
> Shin'd in my Angell-infancy.
> Before I understood this place
> Appointed for my second race,
> Or taught my soul to fancy ought
> But a white, Celestiall thought,
> When yet I had not walkt above
> A mile, or two, from my first love,
> And looking back (at that short space,)
> Could see a glimpse of his bright-face;
> When on some gilded Cloud, or flowre
> My gazing soul would dwell an houre,
> And in those weaker glories spy
> Some shadows of eternity.[62]

Derived from many sources, the Renaissance conception of child-hood as a recapitulation of the State of Innocence became a dominant theme in English literature. As George Boas has observed, the poets of the seventeenth century "had no need to argue about the innocence of childhood, for everyone probably believed in it without defining it precisely."[63] However, while correct in his assessment of the popularity of this theme, Boas has overlooked certain theological complications, including one argument very much alive at the time, the debate between the Puritans and the neoplatonists on the nature of man. Undercutting any conception of childhood innocence, the Puritans, drawing upon Calvin, emphasized the innate depravity of man, his corrupt state at birth, and his desperate need of God's grace for salvation.

The concept of original sin, a belief of Anglicans as well as Puritans, would seem to contradict the association of childhood with innocence. This concept was, moreover, established Christian dogma, reinforced by centuries of religious teachings from the time of St. Augustine, who emphasized man's natural depravity in his Confessions and stated flatly in the Enchiridion that "all those born through carnal lust" have "entered into the inheritance of original sin."[64] Anselmus, in Man in Glory, also denied that any man" (after Adam) did ever taste of" the joys of Eden.[65] In the Renaissance Calvin stated in his commentary on Genesis (1576) that "men are borne evill: . . . so soone as by age they were ripe to thinke, they have a corrupt root of the mind"[66] and the Homilies reminded men repeatedly that "by breaking God's commandment in our first parent [Adam, we] are all become unclean. . . . We are by nature the children of God's wrath."[67] Thomas Wilson and other clergymen of his time pointed dramatically to the "hereditarie disease, called commonly original sin, or birth-sinne, [which has] spread over our whole kind, as a Leprosie, and hath tainted the whole race of us,"[68] and John Woolton denounced those religious sects that emphasized man's inherent goodness: "The Pelagians and certayne Scholemen dreamed mannes nature to bee syncere and uncorrupte after hys Nativitie, even as Adam was before his fall. But that furor is directly agaynst the worde of God: Beholde I am conceyved in iniquitie."[69]

It is true that the Pelagians had considered new-born infants in the same condition as Adam before the Fall.[70] However, the theme of child-hood innocence in the Renaissance was too widespread to have been merely the offshoot of a fifth-century religious heresy. The answer is actually quite simple: when orthodox theologians of the time referred to the innocence of children, presumably these were baptised children. According to Catholic doctrine, the baptismal rite frees infants from original sin and restores them to a state of grace or innocence, and most Protestant theologians agreed with this belief.[71] For example, Donne asked in one of his sermons, "What would a soule oppressed with the sense of sin give, that she were in that state of Innocency that she had in Baptisme?"[72] And Edmund Bonner stated that "the Sacrament of Baptysme alone . . . is sufficiente to salvation, and to bring them to heaven, if in that state of innocencye recovered and gotten by baptysme, they shoulde by and by depart this world."[73] Henry Vaughan's poem, "The Burial of an Infant" underscores his belief in the innocence of childhood (whether inherent or regained in baptism):

> Blest Infant Bud, whose Blossome-life
> Did only look about, and fal,
> Wearyed out in a harmless strife
> Of tears, and milk, the food of all;
> Sweetly didst thou expire: Thy soul
> Flew home unstain'd by his new Kin,
> For ere thou know'st how to be foul,
> Death wean'd thee from the world, and sin.

(II. 1-8)

Thus, for many Renaissance minds, the child became a symbol of Adam before the Fall. As John Earle so eloquently put it in <u>Microcosmographie,</u>

A Child

> Is a man in small letter, yet the best copy of Adam before he tasted of Eve, or the apple. . . . He is purely happy, because he knows no evil, nor hath made means by sin to be acquainted with misery. He arrives not at the mischief of being wise, nor endures evils to come, by forseeing them. He kisses and loves all, and when the smart of the rod is past, smiles on his beater. Nature and his parents alike dandle him, and tice him on with a bait of sugar to a draught of wormwood. He plays yet like a young prentice the first day, and is not come to his task of melancholy. His hardest labour is his tongue, as if he were loath to use so deceitful an organ; and he is best company with it when he can but prattle. We laugh at his foolish sports, but his game is our earnest: and his drums, rattles, and hobby-horses, but the emblems, and mocking of man's business. His father hath writ him as his own little story, wherein he reads those days of his life that he cannot remember; and sighs to see what innocence he has out-lived. The elder he grows, he is a stair lower from God; and like his first father much worse in his breeches. He is the Christian's example and the old man's relapse: the one imitates his pureness, and the other falls into his simplicity. Could he put off his body with his little coat, he had got eternity without a burden & exchanged but one heaven for another.[74]

The child, for Earle and his contemporaries, was a living allegory, a hieroglyph "of Adam before he tasted of Eve, or the apple." Free from all perturbations of spirit and uncorrupted by the materialism around him, the child, they believed, was "purely happy because he knows no evil." Intuitive, innocent, and trusting, he was not yet beset by worry. He had no responsibilities, no obligations, but "play[ed] yet like a young prentice the

21

first day, and [was] not come to his taske of melancholy." Sheltered by his tender age, he saw none of the world's evils and was temporarily free from the curse of arduous labor later imposed on Adam. Laughing delightedly at the world he perceived, the child seemed to be living in a state of "innocence," as close to edenic perfection as this fallen world could bring him.

NOTES

[1] See Henri Baudet, Paradise on Earth, trans. Elizabeth Wentholt (New Haven: Yale Univ. Press, 1965), p. 58 and A. Bartlet Giamatti, The Earthly Paradise and the Renaissance Epic (Princeton: Princeton Univ. Press, 1966), p. 3.

[2] Works and Days, in Hesiod: The Homeric Hymns and Homerica, trans. Hugh G. Evelyn-White (London: Heinemann, 1959), p. 11, ll. 109-20.

[3] For a further discussion of the pastoral, see John Armstrong, The Paradise Myth (London: Oxford Univ. Press, 1969), p. 102 ff. and Edwin Honig, The Dark Conceit: The Making of Allegory (Evanstown: Northwestern Univ. Press, 1959), pp. 163-64.

[4] Baudet, p. 74.

[5] Purgatorio, in The Divine Comedy of Dante Alighieri, trans. John Aitkin Carlyle and Philip H. Wicksteed (New York: Random House, 1950), canto xxviii, p. 361.

[6] The History of the World (London, 1614), p. 38.

[7] The Fall of Man (London, 1616), II, 399.

[8] Giamatti, p. 4.

[9] Arnold Williams, The Common Expositor (Chapel Hill: Univ. of North Carolina Press, 1948), p. 97.

[10] Ralegh, pp. 34-35.

[11] Ralegh, p. 64.

[12] As Williams notes, there was still much speculation in the Renaissance on the exact location of Eden, although "the consensus of nearly all opinion of the Renaissance, including the commentaries, was that Eden, of which Paradise was a part, was somewhere between Palestine and Persia. Pareus lists among other conjectures these: the field of Babylon; all of Syria, Arabia and Mesopotamia; Syria about Damascus; the upper part of Chaldea; Armenia, Syria, Assyria and Egypt; Mesopotamia. The last, Mesopotamia alone, was by all odds the favorite location of Paradise" (p. 99).

[13]Quoted in John Salkeld, A Treatise of Paradise (London, 1617), p. 12.

[14]Salkeld, pp. 14-15.

[15]Certaine Plaine, briefe, and comfortable Notes, upon every Chapter of Genesis (London, 1596), p. 12.

[16]Although in Paradise Lost Adam and Eve are assigned the task of gardening, their cultivation of nature, as Milton depicted it, is partly a pleasure, for it exposes them to the fragrant beauty of paradise.

[17]Salkeld, p. 237.

[18]A Christian Dictionary (London, 1630), s.v. "Innocency."

[19]The Principall Grounds of Christian Religion (London, 1625), p. 5. A gloss on Genesis 1:27 in The Bible: Translated according to the Ebrew and Greeke, and conferred with the best translations in divers Languages (London, 1600) elaborates on the details of this spiritual image and John Ball's discussion in A Short Treatise Contayning all the Principall Grounds of Christian Religion (London, 1631), p. 61, also concurs with this description.

[20]The Guide Unto True Blessednesse (London, 1625), p. 18.

[21]Henry Ainsworth, Annotations Upon the first book of Moses, called Genesis (London, 1616), sig. Blv.

[22]Williams, pp. 73-74.

[23]Ralegh, p. 23.

[24]Fletcher, The History of the Perfect-Cursed-Blessed Man (London, 1629), p. 8.

[25]Meditations on the Six Days of the Creation (1717). Intro. George Robert Guffey. Augustan Repr. Soc. Pub. No. 119. (Los Angeles: William Andrews Clark Memorial Library, 1966), p. 83.

[26]The Summa Theologica. Literally translated by the Fathers of the English Dominican Province (London: Burns, Oates & Washbourne, 1921), XIII, 253.

[27]"Sermon Preached at a Marriage" on Hosea 2.19, May 30, 1621 in The Sermons of John Donne, ed. George R. Potter and Evelyn M. Simpson (Berkeley: Univ. of California Press, 1953-1962), III, 246. All references to Donne's sermons are taken from this edition.

[28]Anthroposophia Theomagica: Or a Discourse of the Nature of Man and his state after death. By Eugenius Philalethes (London, 1650), p. 36.

23

[29] A Profitable and Necessarie Doctrine (London, 1555), sig. A4.

[30] The Practical Christian (London, 1670), p. 133.

[31] Paradise Lost, in The Works of John Milton, ed. Frank Allen Patterson et al. (New York: Columbia Univ. Press, 1931), II. All quotations from Paradise Lost are from this edition and will hereafter be noted in the text.

[32] Aquinas, IV, 306.

[33] Peters Teares: A Sermon Preached at St. Maries Spittle, the xv of April 1612 (London, 1612), p. 15.

[34] Salkeld, pp. 188-89.

[35] Williams, p. 82.

[36] George Boas, The Cult of Childhood (London: Warburg Institute, 1966), p. 18.

[37] A Newe Anatomie of Whole Man (London, 1576), sig. Alv.

[38] Woolton, sig. A3.

[39] The Holy Pilgrime, Leading the Way to New Jerusalem (London, 1609), p. 52.

[40] Bartlet, p. 134.

[41] A Treatise of Security (London, 1622), p. 4.

[42] Williams, p. 107.

[43] Trans. Boethius Bk. I metrum 5 in Olor Iscanus, in The Works of Henry Vaughan, ed. L.C. Martin (Oxford: Clarendon Press, 1957), p. 83. All quotations from Henry Vaughan are taken from this edition and will be noted in the text.

[44] Goodman, II, 399.

[45] Babington, p. 12.

[46] Bartlet, p. 42.

[47] Pious Annotations Upon the Holy Bible (London, 1651), sig. Dlv.

[48] Areopagitica, in Complete Prose Works of John Milton, ed. Douglas Bush et al. (New Haven: Yale Univ. Press, 1959), II, 527.

[49]Enchiridion Ethicum, the English translation of 1690 reproduced from the first edition (New York: Facsimile text society, 1930), p. 6.

[50]Goodman, II, 399.

[51]Diodati, sig. A4 (italics reversed).

[52]The Enclosed Garden (Madison: Univ. of Wisconsin Press, 1966), p. 128.

[53]The New Schaff-Herzog Encyclopedia of Religious Knowledge, ed. Samuel Macauley Jackson et al. (Grand Rapids: Baker Book House, 1963-67), s.v. "Paradise," p. 348.

[54]Paradise, in Hexameron, Paradise, and Cain and Abel, trans. John Savage (New York: Fathers of the Church, 1961), p. 294.

[55]Ralegh, p. 34.

[56]For further discussion on this subject, see Boas, p. 11 ff.

[57]Centuries of Childhood, trans. Robert Baldick (New York: Alfred E. Knopf, 1962), p. 50.

[58]Boas, p. 48.

[59]Titus Burkhardt, Alchemy, trans. William Stoddart (Baltimore: Penguin Books, 1971), p. 125.

[60]The Divine Pymander of Hermes Mercurius Trismegistus (London, 1650), pp. 51-52.

[61]The Paradise Within: Studies in Vaughan, Traherne and Milton (New Haven: Yale Univ. Press, 1964), pp. 26-27.

[62]From Silex Scintillans in Works, pp. 419-20.

[63]Boas, p. 41.

[64]Enchiridion, in Augustine: Confessions and Enchiridion, trans. Albert C. Outler (London: SCM Press, 1955), p. 354.

[65]Man in Glory: Or a Discourse of the blessed estate of the Saints in the New Jerusalem (1652), trans. Henry Vaughan, in Works, p. 200.

[66]A Commentarie of John Calvin Upon the first booke of Moses called Genesis, trans. Thomas Tymme (London, 1578), p. 213.

[67]"Second Part of the Sermon on the Misery of Man," in Certaine Sermons or Homilies appointed to be Read in Churches in the Time of the

<u>Late Queen Elizabeth of Famous Memory</u> (1623), (Oxford: Univ. Press, 1844), pp. 14-15.

[68]<u>A Commentary on the most Divine Epistle of S. Paul to the Romanes</u> (London, 1627), p. 157.

[69]Woolton, sig. D2.

[70]Daniel Featley in <u>Pelagius Redivivus</u> (London, 1626), p. 1, provides a seventeenth-century account of the Pelagian heresy:

1. The sinne of <u>Adam</u> is not imputed to his posteritie

2. <u>Adam</u> by his sinne endamaged onely himselfe properly, but his Posteritie onely by his example, so farre forth as they imitate him.

3. There is no Originall sinne, corruption of humane nature.

4. Every man is borne in the same perfection wherein <u>Adam</u> was before his fall, save onely the perfection of age, which in his posteritie wants the use of reason, when they are new borne.

[71]<u>The Oxford Dictionary of the Christian Church</u>, ed. F.L. Cross (London: Oxford Univ. Press, 1937), s.v. "Infant Baptism," pp. 689-90.

[72]"Sermon Preached at St. Pauls" on 2 Cor. 8.20, <u>Sermons</u>, X, 138-39.

[73]Bonner, sigs. K4v-01.

[74]<u>Micro-Cosmographie</u> (1628), ed. Edward Arber (facsimile reproduction of the first edition) (London: English Reprints, 1869), pp. 21-22.

The State of Misery

28

CHAPTER III

THE STATE OF MISERY

The Historical Concept

To the Renaissance mind, the current state of the world was a direct consequence of the Fall. As Samuel Crooke stated in The Guide Unto True Blessednesse, this "state of corruption and misery" was "the fearfull condition where-unto in Adam all mankinde fell, by transgressing and violating the covenant of workes."[1] Adam's disobedience "did by sinne, disinherite himselfe and his of the infinite treasure of Gods favour: and did thereby purchase a life, whose dayes are consumed in vexations and miserable change; and whose end doth not end his misery; but renew and inlarge it with addition and perpetuity of torment,"[2] Christopher Lever explained in The Holy Pilgrim, adding that the State of Misery "is familiarly knowne in the experience of every mans life; the most fortunate of every mans life being full of the markes of this misery."[3]

Thus, the State of Misery, also known as the State of Nature or Wrath, was seen by the majority of Renaissance theoreticians as the natural condition of postlapsarian mankind. According to Stephen Egerton in A Briefe Method of Catechising, "the estate of every naturall man" is "very miserable and in no wise to be rested in."[4] In The Principal Grounds of Christian Religion, Nicholas Byfield explained, "concerning mans estate of Misery," that "all men by nature, are in a most miserable case, being all deprived of the glory of God."[5] All people are born "in the state of condemnation" explained Arthur Dent in A Plaine Mans Path-Way to Heaven, and echoing the Sermon of Misery in the Homilies, Dent emphasized that "Wee are by nature the children of wrath."[6] Applying this theological premise to seventeenth-century political theory, Thomas Hobbes stated in the Leviathan that "the natural condition of mankind" is a state of "war where every man is enemy to every man," amid "continual fear and danger of violent death; and the life of man solitary, poor, nasty, brutish, and short."[7] Men and women were by nature beasts, governed solely by their own appetites; the only remedy to this natural chaos, Hobbes maintained, was a contrived system of order, an artificial Leviathan of government designed to keep us from destroying one another.

Despite the positive humanism of philosophers like Pico della Mirandola and the appeal of the Pelagian heresy, discussions of natural depravity and original sin clearly predominated in Renaissance descriptions of human nature. As Thomas Jackson stated in A Treatise of the Divine

29

Essence, "Originall sinne is the estate or condition of the sons of wrath, which estate every child of Adam by participation of the first sin doth inherit."[8] Attempting to offer a logical explanation for original sin, theologians like John Bartlet emphasized that Adam's fate, like that of a king, descended upon all of his people: "He was the Father, and Root of all Man-Kind, and receiv'd whatsoever good he had, not only for himself, but all his Posterity. Had he stood in obedience, he and his had continued in that blessed Estate, wherein they were created, but now falling from that by his Rebellion, he brought the Curse upon himself and all his Posterity."[9]

According to most Protestant theologians, each man and woman was born into this miserable state and destined to be judged under God's covenant of works, where they would most certainly be found guilty and condemned to Hell unless they experienced a personal conversion to Christ. Convinced of this, scores of ministers urged their followers to repent, portraying their sinful state with color and vehemence. "Hasten as fast as you can out of the Suburbs of Hell, I mean, your natural unregenerate estate, an estate of ignorance, unbelief, impenitency, disobedience, for this is the broad way to Hell," urged John Bartlet.[10] And Nehemiah Rogers warned his people in The True Convert, "let all wicked unregenerate men take notice of their estate and be warned of their misery, for they are but dead corpses, lying rotting in the graves of iniquitie."[11]

"Taking notice of" the State of Misery involved meditating on its causes and effects, both of which were carefully scrutinized by Renaissance theologians, who studied their own motivations in the process. Jacob Boehme, among others, equated original sin with selfishness, a separation of the individual will from the harmony of the universe. In Signatura Rerum he concluded, "All Sins arise from Self," and "Every Will which entereth into its Self-hood, and seeketh the ground of its Life's Form, the same breaketh it self off from the Great Mystery, and entereth into a Self-fulness, it will be its own (or of its own self-ful Jurisdiction,) and so it is Contrary to the first Mystery, for the Same is alone All; and this Child is accounted evil, for it striveth in disobedience against its own Mother which hath brought it forth."[12] St. Augustine had also described the Fall as a division of consciousness. "The Fall of Man," according to Augustine, was "the result of the 'lower reason' throwing off the control of the 'higher,' and devoting itself to the pursuit of the material and the temporal. Man seeks to be his own master, to have private possessions instead of his share in the universal good."[13] For Thomas Traherne, as well, the Fall signified a selfish fragmentation of experience, a concentration on the part instead of the whole. As he said in the Centuries: "I offended in an apple against Him that gave me the whole World" (C I:75).[14]

According to Boehme, this separation and intense self-absorption were primarily responsible for human misery. "Thou art a rebellious, stubborn, disobedient Child, [who] hast made thy self thine own enemy," Boehme declared of fallen mankind. "Thou canst not dwell in the first Mother, but in thy Self; for thy Will is entered into Self-hood, and all that doth vex, plague, and annoy thee, is only thy Self-hood; thou makest thy self thy own Enemy, and bringest thy self into Self-destruction or Death."[15] A person in the State of Misery was, for Boehme and his contemporaries, a soul divided--both from the world and from a true awareness of himself. As Thomas Jackson realized, a fallen soul's self-centered perception only augments his misery and isolation: the "secret consciousness of our own unlovelinesse, in the state of nature, makes us ofttimes too mistrustful of others love."[16] Suspicious of others, frustrated by an unsympathetic universe, postlapsarian men and women find themselves estranged from the world around them. Countless writers in the sixteenth and seventeenth centuries stressed this sense of alienation while describing the plight of fallen mankind. John Calvin observed that "when Adam fell from his estate, he was by that departure estranged from God";[17] Henry Lok wrote sonnets about "The exild captive-state of sinfull man";[18] and Henry Vaughan complained of his outcast state throughout Silex Scintillans.

Relating personally to their subject, many hexaemeral writers described the Garden of Eden with nostalgia and regret, grieving as they related the story of the Fall. Such was Milton's response as he changed his notes to tragic in Paradise Lost. Such also was the reaction of Du Bartas at the conclusion of the Devine Weekes, where he declared, "Alas, we know what Orion of griefe / Raind on the curst head of the creatures Chiefe."[19] And in his Meditations on the Six Days of the Creation, Thomas Traherne lamented the fall of the angels even as he praised the creation of light, seeing in their apostasy a prelude to ours:

But, O my Soul, see here an Eclipse of these glorious
Spirits of Light.

See here the Mutability and Uncertainty of all created
Beings.

See here, and tremble at what the best are, without
the supporting Hand of divine Providence.

Behold the miserable Effects of Pride and Ingratitude,
that not being contented with such a glorious State, they
did apostatize into the very worst of all possible Beings,
and now remain in Darkness for ever.[20]

In The Historie of the Perfect-Cursed-Blessed Man, Joseph Fletcher described the estate of fallen mankind with obvious emotion:

O cursed Man! Ô miserable wight!
On whom all plagues of Hell, Earth, Heav'n are light.
Both what He hath without, or Him within,
Are all ore-thrown through guilt of deadly Sin.
Look-on his person; look-on his estate;
That's totally deprav'd; this desperate.
So that He must in grievous miserie
First spend his daies; then die eternally.[21]

31

As Fletcher has shown, the effects of the Fall on man were two-fold: corrupting "Both what He hath without, or Him within." In Eden the individual had been at peace with himself and his world; the State of Innocence had been a condition of total harmony. The State of Misery was, on the other hand, a state of division. In the biblical account, Adam and Eve were cast out of paradise and the knowledge of good and evil divided their previously unified sensibilities. Their new awareness of self brought suffering in its wake. Henceforth men were to labor for existence and women to suffer in childbirth. The interaction of self and environment was to be, for mankind, an often painful conflict.

The Fall brought with it a sense of time and initiated the course of human history. What had been heretofore an experience of two immortal beings in an eternal garden of pleasure became fragmented by time and change. Nothing remained constant under the moon, according to Renaissance cosmology. Beauty, joy, and life itself were fleeting; all was subject to the law of mutability. As John Woolton declared in A New Anatomie of Whole Man:

> Man hath also lost eternall felicitie and blessednesse,
> and hath onely left unto him in steede thereof, this
> worldly and earthly lyfe: which is short, miserable, &
> painefull, and is subject to daungerous death every mo-
> ment. . . . the shortnes of mans lyfe, the perils & dan-
> gers in the same, the cruel diseases, the untimely, soden,
> & unnatural deathes, & the resolution of our bodies into
> dust & ashes, ... Which thinges I willingly note, to
> admonishe men deeply to consider their miserable and
> wretched estate.[22]

Renaissance commentators like Edward Bonner and Godfrey Goodman pointed to the Book of Job as emblematic of the State of Misery. According to Bonner, "the holye prophet Job, havynge in hym selfe great experience of the miserable and synnefull estate of man, dothe open the same to the worlde in these wordes. . . . Man beyng borne of a woman, lyvynge a short tyme, is full of manyfolde miseries, hy spryngeth up lyke a flower, & fadeth againe, vanyshynge away (as it were) as shadow, and never contineweth in one state."[23] In a similar vein, Goodman wrote, "Me thinkes I see the state and condition of every man, lively set forth in the first Chapter of Job: Whersoever, or howsoever the wind blowes, from any quarter of the world, it still serves to bring us some heavie tidings, concerning our selves, our health, our children, our kindred, our substance, our servants: all are subject to shipwracke, every thing falles to decay."[24]

Mutability was seen as part of the death sentence imposed on us by the Fall. According to Robert Bruce, Scottish theologian of the 1590's death was the ultimate division, "a violent twinning and rugging syndrie, of the quhilk the Lord hath appoynted to byde together, to wit, the soule and the bodie: . . . by reason of disobedience & breaking of the law of God, in came sin, in commeth the violent separation, in commeth death, quhilk is the reward of sin."[25] Jeremy Taylor, like Thomas Aquinas, defined death as the slow corruption or mutability engendered from the moment of the Fall. In Holy Living he explained that "Death is not an action, but a whole state and condition; and this was first brought in upon us by the offense of one man . . . when he fell . . . upon that very day he fell into an evil and dangerous condition, a state of change and affliction; then death began, that is, the man began to die by a natural diminution, and aptness to disease and misery. His first state was, and should have been so long as it lasted, a happy duration; his second was a daily and miserable change, and this was the dying properly."[26]

The effects of the Fall on the human soul were discussed at length by theologians. Essentially, men and women lost the intuitive wisdom, grace, and perfection of Innocence, falling from inner harmony to discord. Because of the Fall they were dispossessed and disinherited of their "Native dignity by Creation." Created only a "little lower than the Angels," man by his Fall became "lower than the Beasts. . . . By this he lost his honourable title, as the Child of God."[27] Deprived of the grace that had been theirs at Creation, fallen mankind degenerated in both body and soul. As Edmund Bonner explained, "the whole nature of man, both in bodye and soule, was through orygynall synne, greatelye defiled. For the soule (which is the chief part of man) loste thereby the especiall gyftes of grace, with which it was indued in the creation, and besydes that, it was also maymed in the gyftes of nature, as in memorye, intelligence, wyll, and other lyke."[28] The balanced mind of Adam before the Fall became the tempest-tossed mind of postlapsarian man, in whom passions run wild and "reason panders will."

Misled by their corrupt senses, fallen men and women were seen as wandering in spiritual darkness, ignorant of the light of truth. As Paul Bayne concluded, man "under the power of the Divell, the Prince of darknesse, [is] in all kinds of darknesse; . . . darknesse of ignorance, none understandeth, none seeketh after God: darknesse of Lusts and ungodlinesse."[29] Misery was defined by St. Augustine as not merely darkness but spiritual blindness. "This was in fact the root of my misery," he declared in the Confessions, "that I was so fallen and blinded that I could not discern the light of virtue and of beauty."[30] Traherne also equated Misery with fallen apprehension. Fallen men, "corrupt in their Understandings, . . . are narrow and base and servile in their Affections. They start at a shadow, and boggle at a feather. Sin hath transformed them into Slaves and Cowards. They misapprehend the Nature of their Duty like Fools; that were made to be great and Mighty as Kings" (CE, p. 85).

The painful effects of the Fall infected not only human beings as Renaissance theologians reiterated, but the entire world. Godfrey Goodman reminded his readers that "the greatnesse of our woe shewes the large extent of our sinne: this world which we inhabit, is but a painted miserie."[31] Everywhere they looked, all around them, people were confronted by the evidence of the Fall. As Traherne explained in Christian Ethicks,

33

all things before his fall were subservient to mans Glory and
blessedness, so all things after his fall became opposite to
him; all creatures up braided him with him Guilt, every thing
aggravated his Sin and increased his Damnation. The glory
and Blessedness which he lost was his Torment, the Honour
which he had before, was turned into shame; the Love of
GOD, which he had offended, increased his Guilt. Eternity
was a Horror to him, his Conscience a Tormentor, and his
Life a Burden; Nothing but shame and Despair could follow
his Sin, the Light of nature it selfe condemned him, and
all that he could see was, that he was deformed, and hated
of God.[32]

   The world had not only been immediately corrupted by the Fall, but
it was believed to be in a state of progressive decay. As a modern scholar has pointed out, the theory of the decay of nature was an integral
part of Renaissance cosmology, and the increased concentration on their
spiritual identity brought about a growing concern over the degeneration
of the world.[33] The two were seen as emblematic parallels: in the world's
ills was a mirror image of the ills of mankind. John Donne portrayed
this relationship in his "First Anniversary," observing that

        as mankinde, so is the worlds whole frame
        Quite out of joynt. . . .
        . . . .
        The noblest part, man, felt it first; and than
        Both beasts and plants, curst in the curse of man.
        So did the world from the first houre decay,
        The evening was beginning of the day,
        And now the Springs and Sommers which we see,
        Like sonnes of women after fiftie bee.
        And new Philosophy cals all in doubt,
        The Element of fire is quite put out;
        The Sun is lost, and th'earth, and no mans wit
        Can well direct him where to looke for it.
        And freely men confesse, that this world's spent,
        When the Planets, and the Firmament
        They seeke so many new; they see that this
        Is crumbled out againe to' his Atomies
        'Tis all in peeces, all cohaerence gone.

                            (ll. 191-213)[34]

Thomas Traherne, as well, emphasized the parallel decay of macrocosm
and microcosm:

        Mankind is sick, the World distemper'd lies,
            Opprest with Sins and Miseries.
        Their Sins are Woes; a long corrupted Train
            Of Poyson, drawn from Adam's vein,
            Stains all his Seed, and all his Kin

34

Are one Disease of Life within.
           They all torment themselves!
The World's one <u>Bedlam</u>, or a greater Cave
Of Mad-men, that do alwaies rave.

("Mankind is Sick," ll. 1-9)[35]

Shaken from complacency by recent geographical and scientific discover-
ies which dispossessed the Ptolomaic universe and called into question the
medieval world view, people in the Renaissance found themselves cast into
further uncertainty as the world around them seemed to degenerate before
their very eyes. Exiled from certitude, lost in confusion, these souls in
the State of Misery groped for truth amid a world of darkness and decay.

Misery and Individual Experience

As we have seen, the religious writers of the Renaissance regarded
the pain and confusion of their world as direct evidence of their fallen
state. However, many of them also believed, with St. Augustine, that the
individual recapitulated the Fall in his own lifetime, moving from a state
of relative innocence in early childhood into a far more serious state of
sin with the dawn of reason and self-awareness. Thomas Jackson discussed
this progression within the individual in <u>A Treatise of the Primaeval Estate of the First Man</u>. "Actually to transgress after the similitude of
<u>Adam</u>, Infants, whilst Infants, cannot," he explained. "For <u>such Transgres-
sion consists in a sinister choice of the Will</u>; of in the use of Reason,
which cannot be in Infants." Protected initially by baptism, infants exist
in a state of relative innocence until "their first Arrival unto the use of
Reason, or at their Passage out of Infancy into Youth, [when they] are
under <u>This Yoke</u>. . . . All must of necessity have Original Sin or some
Reliques as will impell them to some Actuall Sin or other, or to some
transgression of some of Gods Commandments, when they come unto the
Use of Reason."[36] Acknowledging that the growth of the individual from
infancy to the age of reason represented a fall from security to uncertainty, John Earle also noted the psychological changes within the individual.
He observed in <u>Micro-Cosmographie</u> that a youth is in a precarious state,
subject to corruption by the world and by his own desires.

> Hee is now out of Natures protection, though not yet able To
> guide himselfe: But left loose to the World, and Fortune, from
> which the weaknesse of his Childhood preserv'd him: and now
> his strength exposes him. Hee is indeed just of age to be
> miserable, yet in his owne conceit first begins to be happy;
> . . . . He sees yet but the outside of the World and Men, and
> conceives them according to their appealing glister, and out
> of this ignorance beleeves them. He pursues all vanities for
> happinesse, and enjoys them best in this fancy. His reason
> serves not to curbe, but understand his appetite, and prose-
> cute the motions thereof with a more eager earnestnes. Him-
> selfe is his own temptation, and needs not Satan; and the World

35

will come hereafter. . . . Everie action is his danger, and every
man his ambush. Hee is a Shippe without Pilot or Tackling,
and only good fortune may steere him. If hee scape this age,
he ha's scap't a Tempest, and may live to be a Man.

According to Earle, then, a youth is extremely vulnerable. Deprived of
his childhood innocence and intuitive powers, he is misled by appearances,
"sees yet but the outside of the World and Men." Not only does the world
mislead him, but he misleads himself, with fallen senses and fallen reason.
Deprived of his inner light, fallen from truth, "Hee is a Shippe without
Pilot or Tackling," set adrift upon the rough seas of the fallen world.

In "Affliction (I)" George Herbert described such a progression from
innocence to alienation, relating how the increasing years brought with
them increasing misery:

> At first thou gav'st me milk and sweetnesses;
> I had my wish and way:
> My dayes were straw'd with flow'rs and happinesse;
> There was no moneth but May.
> But with my yeares sorrow did twist and grow,
> And make a partie unawares for wo.
> My flesh began unto my soul in pain,
> Sicknesses cleave my bones;
> Conspiring agues dwell in ev'ry vein,
> And tune my breath to grones.
> Sorrow was all my Soul; I scarce beleeved,
> Till grief did tell me roundly, that I lived.

Fallen from the springtime of his life, he found himself "entangled in the
world of strife," sadly aware of his postlapsarian state.[38]

Henry Vaughan depicted his fall into misery in "Distraction," where,
like Herbert, he realized:

> I find my selfe the lesse, the more I grow;
> The world
> Is full of voices; Man is call'd, and hurl'd
> By each. . . .

(ll. 10-13)

In a later stanza he called out to God to save him from this world of
confusion:

> Lest left alone too long
> Amidst the noise and throng.
> Oppressed I
> Striving to save the whole, by parcells dye.

(ll. 31-34)[39]

36

The sense of exile, of a soul lost in darkness crying out for relief, informs much of Vaughan's work. In "The Pilgrimage" he stated:

> So for this night I linger here,
> And full of tossings too and fro,
> Expect stil when thou wilt appear.

(ll. 9-11)

And in "The Ass" he cried out:

> break or untye
> These bonds, this sad captivity,
> This leaden state, which men miscal
> Being and life, but is dead thrall.

(ll. 53-56)

Yet the desolation, fear, and uncertainty experienced in the State of Misery were regarded by Vaughan, Herbert, and other religious writers of the time as a painful but necessary part of regeneration. For as their French contemporary Pascal had pointed out, acknowledging the agonizing reality of misery was far better than remaining in darkness and ignorance. According to Pascal, people pursue a continuous round of diversions to distract them from the lack of fulfillment in this life. And yet diversion "is the greatest of our miseries. For it . . . prevents us from thinking about ourselves and leads us imperceptibly to destruction. But for that we should be bored, and boredom would drive us to seek some more solid means of escape, but diversion passes our time and brings us imperceptibly to our death."[40] Thus, instead of continuing to ignore their miserable estate, parishioners were counseled by their pastors to focus on it, to recognize the instability and disappointments of this fallen world and to seek instead the eternal realm of the spirit. Within the larger pattern, then, meditation on the State of Misery was seen as an effective spiritual exercise, which could lead the soul through a dark night of penance into the dawn of the State of Grace.

NOTES

[1] The Guide Unto True Blessednesse (London, 1625), p. 21.

[2] The Holy Pilgrime, Leading the Way to New Jerusalem (London, 1609), pp. 69-70.

[3] Lever, p. 64.

[4] A Briefe Method of Catechising (London, 1597), p. 20.

[5] The Principall Grounds of Christian Religion (London, 1625), p. 6.

[6]A Plaine Mans Path-way to Heaven (London, 1601), p. 4; Sermon of Misery in Certaine Sermons or Homilies Appointed to be Read in Churches in the Time of the Late Queen Elizabeth of Famous Memory (1623) (Oxford: Oxford Univ. Press, 1844), p. 10.

[7]Leviathan: Parts I and II. Intro. Herbert W. Schneider (New York: Bobbs-Merrill, 1958), pp. 104, 107.

[8]A Treatise of the Divine Essence (London, 1628-29), II, 84.

[9]The Practical Christian (London, 1670), pp. 137-38.

[10]Bartlet, p. 199.

[11]The True Convert (London, 1620), p. 284.

[12]Signatura Rerum: or the Signature of all Things (London, 1651), pp. 180, 179.

[13]Augustine: Later Works, ed. and trans. John Burnaby (Philadelphia: Westminster Press, 1955), p. 93.

[14]Centuries of Meditations in Centuries, Poems, and Thanksgivings, ed. H.M. Margoliouth (Oxford: Clarendon Press, 1955), I. All references to the Centuries (C) are from this edition and will be abbreviated in the text.

[15]Boehme, p. 179.

[16]Jackson, II, 204.

[17]Calvin, The Institution of Christian Religion, written in Latine by M. John Calvine, and Translated into English . . . by Thomas Norton (London, 1582), Bk. I, p. 53.

[18]Sonnet LXXX of Sundry Affectionate Sonets of a feeling Conscience in Poems by Henry Lok, Gentleman: (1593-97), Miscellanies of the Fuller Worthies' Library, ed. Alexander B. Grosart (London, 1871), p. 297.

[19]Bartas: His Devine Weekes and Workes Translated: & Dedicated to the Kings most excellent Majestie, by Joshua Sylvester (London, 1605), p. 295.

[20]Meditations on the Six Days of the Creation (1717). Introd. George Robert Guffey. Augustan Repr. Soc. Pub. No. 119 (Los Angeles: William Andrews Clark Memorial Library, 1966), p. 3.

[21]The Historie of the Perfect-Cursed-Blessed Man (London, 1629), p. 32. (Note how the title includes the first three estates.)

[22]A New Anatomie of whole man, as well as of his body, as of his Soule: Declaring the condition and constitution of the same, in his first creation, corruption, regeneration, and glorification (London, 1576), sig. D1. (Note the progression of the four estates in the title.)

[23]A Profitable and Necessary Doctryne, with Certayne Homilies adjoyned thereunto set forth by the reverende father in God, Edmunde, byshop of London(London, 1555), sig. B4.

[24]The Fall of Man or the Corruption of Nature (London, 1616), II, 117.

[25]"The Thrid Sermon upon Isaiah, chp. 38," in Sermons Preached in the Kirk of Edinburgh (Edinburgh, 1591), sig. F7v-F8.

[26]Thomas Aquinas, The Summa Theologica, trans. the Fathers of the English Dominican Province (London: Burns, Vales & Washbourne, 1921), XIII, 166-67; Jeremy Taylor, The Rule and Exercises of Holy Living (1650) in The Whole Works of the Right Rev. Jeremy Taylor, D.D. (London, 1872), III, 309.

[27]Bartlet, pp. 150-51.

[28]Bonner, sig. D.

[29]A Commentarie Upon the First and Second Chapters of Saint Paul to the Colossians (London, 1634), pp. 63-64.

[30]Confessions, in Augustine: Confessions and Enchiridion, trans. Albert C. Outler (London: SCM Press, 1955), p. 133.

[31]Goodman, Epistle Dedicatory, sig. A4.

[32]Christian Ethicks (1675), ed. Carol L. Marks and George R. Guffey (Ithaca: Cornell Univ. Press, 1968), pp. 100-01.

[33]Victor Harris, All Coherence Gone (Chicago: Univ. of Chicago Press, 1949), p. 1.

[34]An Anatomie of the World. Wherein, By occasion of the untimely death of Mistris Elizabeth Drury, the frailty and decay of the whole world is represented, in The Poems of John Donne, ed. Herbert J.C. Grierson (Oxford: Oxford Univ. Press, 1912), I, 237.

[35]Centuries, Poems and Thanksgivings, ed. H.M. Margoliouth (Oxford: Clarendon Press, 1958), II.

[36]A Treatise of the Primaeval Estate of the First Man, in The Works of the Reverend and Learned Divine, Thomas Jackson, D.D. (London, 1673), pp. 99-100.

[37]Micro-Cosmographie (1628), ed. Edward Arber (facsimile reproduction of the first edition) (London: English Reprints, 1869), pp. 50-51.

[38]From The Temple (1633) in The Works of George Herbert, ed. F.E. Hutchinson (Oxford: Clarendon Press, 1941), ll. 19-41.

[39]From Silex Scintillans (1655) in The Works of Henry Vaughan, ed. Leonard Cyril Martin (Oxford: Clarendon Press, 1957). All of Vaughan's poems cited are from this edition.

[40]Pascal: Pensees, trans. A.J. Krailsheimer (Baltimore, Md.: Penguin Books, 1966), p. 148.

Verbera, ſputa, crucem Verbum patitur Caro factum,
Vt viuat Cœlis, morte ſolutus Homo.

The State of Grace

42

CHAPTER IV

THE STATE OF GRACE

The Historical Concept

In the atmosphere of religious intensity that dominated the early
seventeenth century, the State of Grace was a subject of great concern.
Divines like William Perkins counseled their parishioners: "above all
things in this world, let your principall care be to procure unto your
selves the kingdome of God; that is, that state of grace, whereby you
may enjoy Gods favour in Christ,"[1] and John Bartlet reminded people to
meditate frequently and examine their consciences "to see whether you
can finde your selves in a state of grace."[2]

Historically, the State of Grace involved the Redemption of mankind by Jesus Christ from the State of Misery to the new dispensation
which would enable just men to obtain salvation. As Nicholas Byfield
explained in The Principall Grounds of Christian Religion, "the third estate of man, which is the estate of Grace" represented God's election of
"certaine men to eternall Salvation" for which he sent "in the fulnesse of
time. . . his onely begotten Sonne Jesus Christ to Redeeme us from our
misery."[3] In a similar vein, John Diodati stated in his Pious Annotations
Upon the Holy Bible that "God through his infinite mercy restored man
into a new state of grace and hope of life, by the promise of a Saviour."[4]
In Paradise Lost, Milton protrayed Christ's role in the Redemption as a
heroic willingness to undergo death because of his love for mankind. Like
Milton, John Bartlet emphasized "the free unsearchable love and grace of
God . . . , in not leaving his Elect in their fallen cursed condition, but in
his appointed time, effectually calling all such as belong unto his Election of grace, out of a state of nature into a state of grace."[5]

This "Election of grace" was a troublesome doctrine to many six-
teenth- and seventeenth-century theologians. Some, like Daniel Featly
and Thomas Jackson, espoused the strict Calvinist interpretation, in which
all humanity was condemned by the Fall, but out "of his mercy & grace,
[God] chose & chooseth some out of the estate of misery, and corruption;
maketh them his sonnes by adoption, calleth them to the knowledge of
the truth, regenerateth them by his spirit, justifieth them by faith, and
in the end crowneth them with everlasting glory." Others, less fortunate,
remain "in the state of misery and corruption" and are ultimately condemned to "everlasting torments in hell."[6] Milton's view was milder, and
in his description salvation and "offer'd grace" were extended to all, some

43

of whom were given "peculiar grace . . . above the rest."[7] Thomas Traherne, like Milton, emphasized the mercy of God and interpreted election
as merely a special grace given to a few exemplary souls to lead the rest
out of darkness. As he stated in Christian Ethicks, "The Election of GOD
may be more strictly, or Generally conceived. His Election of particular
persons from the Rebellious Mass of Mankind to be employed, as Ministers
in restoring the residue is a matter of Grace; which as Arbitrary and free,
is occasioned by the Accident of their General Rebellion and his Mercy
hereupon."[8]

Despite their different interpretations of Election, Renaissance
Christians agreed that Christ had redeemed mankind from the State of
Misery by taking upon himself man's nature and undergoing suffering and
death. He fulfilled the terms of the Old Covenant by bearing the punishment for sin and initiated the New Covenant of Grace. As Samuel Crooke
described it, this "new Covenant of Grace . . . . Gods second contract
with mankinde, after the fall, [involved] restoring of him into his favour,
and to the state of happinesse, by the meanes of a Mediator."[9] The New
Covenant, John Bartlet explained, differed from the "Covenant of Works,
which God made with Adam in the state of Innocency [in that the first]
promised Life and Salvation, upon condition of doing the whole will of
God; this, only upon condition of believing, and giving God the glory of
his grace in it."[10]

Mankind was redeemed from the misery of the first by the mercy of
the second Adam. This St. Augustine had explained in The City of God:
"for as we all fell into this misery by one man's sin, so shall we ascend
unto that glory by one (deified) Man's righteousness."[11] The typological
conceit of the first and the second Adam was a popular one. John Donne
employed it in his "Hymn to God my God, in my sicknesse":

> We thinke that Paradise and Calvarie,
>   Christs Crosse, and Adams tree, stood in one place;
> Looke Lord, and fine both Adams met in me:
>   As the first Adams sweat surrounds my face,
>   May the last Adams blood my soule embrace.
>
>   (ll. 21-25)[12]

Milton used the conceit in Paradise Lost, as God announced to his Son:

>   Be thou in Adams room
> The Head of all mankind, thou Adams Son.
> As in him perish all men, so in thee
> As from a second root shall be restor'd
> As many as are restor'd, without thee none.
> His crime makes guiltie all his Sons, thy merit
> Imputed shall absolve them who renounce
> Thir own both righteous and unrighteous deeds,
> And live in thee transplanted, and from thee
> Receive new life.   (III: 285-294)

In a variation on this theme, Joseph Beaumont portrayed the cross as another tree of life, a renewal of what was lost in the Fall:

> What help were left, had JESUS'S Pity not
> Shewd me another Tree, which can
> Enliven dying Man.
> That Tree, made Fertile by his own dear blood;
> And by his Death with quick'ning virtue fraught.
> I now dread not the thought
> Of barracado'd Eden, since as good
> A Paradise I planted see
> On open Calvarie.

(ll. 27-35)[13]

Historically, then, as the first Adam had brought mankind into the State of Misery, so in the Redemption Christ brought his people out of Misery into the State of Grace and offered them the promise of salvation.

Grace and Individual Conversion

Although Christ gave mankind the New Covenant and the promise of Redemption, most seventeenth-century Protestants believed that salvation could come to the individual only through a conversion experience, or the reenactment of the Redemption in his own mind and soul. Individuals in this life were believed to be "either in the State of Election or Reprobation."[14] If they had been "saved" they were in the State of Grace; otherwise they remained among the condemned in the State of Misery. In The Plaine Mans Path-way to Heaven, Arthur Dent explained that "men continue in [the] wofull State of nature, being under the curse of the Law, and the very slavery of Sathan and sin . . . till they be regenerate and borne again & so brought into the State of grace."[15] And Richard Bernard in A Double Catechisme stressed that only "the true believers [unlike] the rest of mankind . . . are in the state of grace, they have communion with Christ."[16]

In A Godly and Learned Exposition, William Perkins defined conversion as the experience which "bring[s] a man from spiritual darknes, unto light, from the power of Satan, unto God, from the state of sinne and the dangers of hell fire, to the state of grace in true faith and repentance, and so to life eternall."[17] But how such a conversion was actually brought about became a much-debated question. Traditional Catholic doctrine held that one entered the State of Grace through a combination of faith and good works in the Sacrament of Penance.[18] Reacting against the Catholic emphasis on good works, however, Renaissance Protestants maintained that faith alone was sufficient for salvation. As Stephen Egerton affirmed in A Brief Method of Catechising, "the onely meanes to free us out of this miserable estate, and to make us truely happie and holy, is Jesus Christ alone, and the same apprehendeth only by faith."[19] John Bartlet contended, in like manner, that in the "Covenant of grace nothing

[is] requir'd on our part but only faith, Believe in the Lord Jesus Christ, and thou shalt be saved." [20] In the Homilies the Church of England upheld justification by faith as official doctrine, maintaining to its parishioners:

> Only faith justifieth us; meaning none other thing than St. Paul meant, when he said, Faith without works justifieth us. And because all this is brought to pass through the only merits and deservings of our saviour Christ, and not our own merits, or through the merit of any virtue that we have within us, or of any work that cometh from us; therefore, in that respect of merit and deserving, we forsake, as it were, altogether again, faith, works, and all other virtues. For our own imperfection is so great, through the corruption of original sin, that all is unperfect that is within us, faith, charity, hope, dread, thoughts, words, and works, and therefore not apt to merit and deserve any part of our justification for us. [21]

But was the faith required of us to be active or passive? Could individuals in any way improve their state or was salvation wholly a work of God? On this question, again, there were many opinions, from the Calvinistic approach of Thomas Jackson who held that "our estate of Election . . . is meerly the work of God; we have no finger, no imployment in it," [22] to others like Godfrey Goodman and John Bartlet, who emphasized the power of prayer. Through "invocation and prayer," Goodman contended, "a naturall man can obtaine guidance from the spirit of God, which then leads him to repentance and grace." [23] In the same vein, Bartlet reminded his readers to "remember to beg the Spirit of God to quicken his Word, that it may quicken your dead Souls, whereby you may be enabled to stand up from the dead, and act as new Creatures in a state of Regeneration." [24]

However, despite the doctrinal extremes of the Calvinists on the one hand and the Latitudinarians on the other, conversion, for the majority of Renaissance Protestants, involved a combination of God's grace and human faith. Moreover, they believed that this "transferring of a man out of the state of sin and miserie, into the state of righteousnesse and happinesse," [25] produced a dramatic transformation in personality. Countless spiritual autobiographies and sermons of the time described this revolution in consciousness, and the signs whereby one might recognize his election. For example, in The Righteous Mans Evidence for Heaven Tymothy Rogers testified to his readers that "there is an effectual calling and conversion wrought in mee; for the Lord of his unspeakable goodnesse hath delivered mee out of the power of darknesse, and translated mee into the kingdom of his deare son, that is, hee hath brought mee out of the miserable estate of nature wherein I was borne, into the happy estate of grace wherein now I stand: this calling is a sure signe that one is ordained to everlasting life." [26] So also Joseph Hall in The Balm of Gilead counseled people to examine their consciences, for "The Spirit of God hath a voice, and our soul hath an ear: that voice of the Spirit speaks inwardly, and effectually to the ear of the soul, calling us out of the state of corrupt Nature into the state of Grace; out of darkness into his marvellous light. By thy calling therefore maist thou judge of thine election."[27]

Calling was recognized as the first stage of the conversion experience and was followed by repentance and regeneration.[28] Revealing to men and women their degenerate estate and leading them to repentance and renewal, calling represented God's prevenient grace, as Robert Rollock explained in his Treatise of Calling:

> he inlightneth us by his holy spirit, pouring a new & a heavenly light into our mind before so blind, as that it neither saw, nor could see the things which doe belong to the Spirit of God. I. Cor. 2. 14.15. The naturall man perceiveth not the things of the Spirit of God, for they are foolishnesse unto him, neither can he know them. In the will which is altogether forward and quite fallen from God, he worketh an uprightnesse, and in all the affections a new holinesse. Hence proceedes the new creature, and that new man which is created after God in righteousnesse and true holinesse. Eph. 4.24.[29]

In this first stage of grace, then, God enlightens our fallen senses and repairs our corrupt will. Emphasizing the individual's passivity in the process, Christopher Lever attributed this awakening to the holy ghost, maintaining:

> All grace is the gift of God, and every motion to goodnesse is caused by the spirit of God onely; our selves being meerly passive in all divine exercise, God himselfe being the actor, and principall mover. For as he that learneth to write, hath his hand first led by the direction of his teacher, before he can merit any little commendation: so the holy Ghost (by whose directions we learne the use of all spirituall exercise) doth move both our capacity and power, to understand the knowledge & use of necessary Christian performance.[30]

There was, as one might expect, considerable debate on the subject of prevenient grace. Robert Rollock, for example, was annoyed by any reference to the holy ghost, which represented to him the Catholic emphasis on free will and undermined the significance of God's grace: "The Papists call this first grace in the faith and work of the holy Ghost, . . . This they say then, that after the fall, man retained not only the faculties of his soule, but also the holy qualities of those powers, only hurt and weakened. And this is that free-will, which they say is quickened by Gods preventing grace, which they define to be an externall motion, standing as it were without, and beating at the door of the heart."[31]

Most theologians of the time agreed that calling awakened one's faith and initiated the next stage of repentance, in which one became aware of his fallen state, advancing through the penitential process of

47

conviction, contrition, and confession to the final stage of regeneration. In his Confessions, St. Augustine had described his mortification when God revealed to him his sinful state: "It was pleasing in thy sight to reform my deformity, and by inward stings thou didst disturb me so that I was impatient until thou wert made clear to my inward sight. By the secret hands of thy healing my swelling was lessened, the disordered and darkened eyesight of my mind was from day to day made whole by the stinging salve of wholesome grief."[32] In the seventeenth century, Christopher Lever also emphasized the necessity of such mortification: "He that is resolved to indevour his godly repentance, and laboreth the reformation of his sinfull life, must labour two things principally, and of necessity; the first is Mortification, the next regeneration. He must first destroy his sinfull estate, before he can obtaine the state of grace."[33] Henry Vaughan voiced the same opinion in his poem "Affliction," maintaining that

> Sickness is wholsome, and Crosses are but curbs
>   To check the mule, unruly man,
> They are heavens husbandry, the famous fan
>   Purging the floor which Chaff disturbs.
> Were all the year one constant Sun-shine, wee
>   Should have no flowres,
> All would be drought, and leanness; not a tree
>   Would make us bowres.

(ll. 17-24)[34]

Conviction of one's sinful nature was accompanied by sadness and longing, a "dark night of the soul." Christopher Lever described the contrition that results:

> when Christian men have understanding by the law of God,
> of their miserable estate (in respect of sinne) what they
> were in innocency; what they are in sinne; and what they
> shall be in judgement, it bringeth a general sadnesse on
> the soules of men, and dulleth the spirit and delight they
> have had in their prosperous fortunes. For when God giveth
> grace to any one to examine his life, & to view his own
> deformities, the first knowledge & apprehension of his
> misery is most terrible because his conscience doth forcibly
> check the former proceedings of his life & violently hale
> him against the current of his own affections.[35]

Several of George Herbert's poems in The Temple depict the agony and contrition with which a sick soul cries out to God. In "Longing" he declared:

> With sick and famisht eyes
> With doubling knees and weary bones,
>   To thee my cries
>   To thee my groanes;

To thee my sighs, my tears ascend;
                    No end?
My throat, my soul is hoarse;
My heart is wither'd like a ground
        Which thou dost curse
        My thoughts turn round,
And make me giddie; Lord, I fall,
                    Yet call.
                                        (ll. 1-12)[36]

Many of John Donne's holy sonnets, as well, convey the torment of conviction and contrition. In one sonnet he cried out to God:

Why doth the devill then usurpe on mee?
Why doth he steale, nay ravish that's thy right?
Except thou rise and for thine owne worke fight,
Oh I shall soone despaire, when I doe see
That thou lov'st mankind well, yet wilt not chuse me.
And Satan hates mee, yet is loth to lose mee.
                    ("As due by many titles," ll. 9-14)

In another well-known sonnet, beseiged by legions of devils, he begged God to invade him with his grace and save him from the enemy, the violent imagery and rough meter of this poem attesting to the vehemence of his plea:

Batter my heart, three person'd God: for, you
As yet but knocke, breathe, shine, and seeke to mend;
That I may rise, and stand, o'erthrow mee, 'and bend
Your force, to breake, blowe, burn and make me new.
I, like an usurpt towne, to'another due,
Labour to'admit you, but Oh, to no end,
Reason your viceroy in mee, mee should defend,
But is captiv'd, and proves weake or untrue.
Yet dearely' I love you, 'and would be loved faine,
But am betroth'd unto your enemie;
Divorce mee, 'untie, or breake that knot againe,
Take mee to you, imprison mee, for I
Except you' enthrall me, never shall be free,
Nor ever chast, except you ravish mee.
        ("Batter my heart, three person'd God")

Henry Vaughan's poem "Repentence" portrays the entire progression of conviction, contrition, and confession in the repentant soul. In the first six lines he declared his awareness of his gifts in creation and his miserable state after the Fall, acknowledging his own sinful nature:

Lord, since thou didst in this vile Clay
        That sacred Ray
Thy spirit plant, quickning the whole
With that one grains Infused wealth,

49

My forward flesh creept on, and subtly stole
Both growth and power. . . .

(ll. 1-6)

In the next few lines he reiterated his fault, his responsibility for his misery, and turned to God in contrition:

Wherefore, pierc't through with grief, my sad
Seduced soul sighs up to thee,
To thee who with true light art Clad
And seest all things just as they be.

(ll. 19-22)

Advancing from contrition to confession, he implored God to

Look from thy throne upon this Rowl
Of heavy sins, my high transgressions,
Which I Confesse withall my soul,
My God, Accept of my Confession.

(ll. 23-26)

Purified by penance and grief, the soul is prepared for regeneration, the final stage of the conversion process. As one's suffering recedes, he becomes conscious of "a contrary estate" of great joy and radiance, perceiving, according to Isaac Pennington, "A way of redemption from al this death, darkness, slavery and misery, and an estatement into that which hath in it a contrary excellency unto it all. Sin shall be done away, the soul shall be made free from it: There is a mighty Saviour which hath a salvation to dispense, which wil set at liberty from al these." [37] As John Bartlet has explained, this experience is sanctifying grace, "otherwise call'd in the Scripture Regeneration, John 3.6. and Renovation of the Image of God, Eph. 4.24 and Sanctification of the whole Man, I Thes. 5.23." [38] For John Woolton this represented a wonderful and mysterious renewal of the entire individual:

whereby our mercifull God doth spiritually forme and fashion
of a carnal man, a newe, just, and holy manne, ingrafting
him into his kingdome, removing from hym his sinnes committed, his wrath & indignation, and imparteth unto him his justice & grace: delivereth him also from the power and kingdome of the Divell, and giveth him the holye ghost, the
earnest pledge of eternall lyfe: and fynallye kindleth in him
newe strength to begin newnes of life, acceptable and pleasant unto God in this world. [39]

By regeneration one is reborn as a "sonne of God, the temple of the holy ghost, and an heire of eternall life." [40]

That one must be "born again" to enter the Kingdom of Heaven was a familiar biblical injunction, cited by High Anglicans as well as Calvinists like Thomas Jackson, who maintained that "in every son of <u>Adam</u>, which in time becomes the <u>Son of God</u>, there must be a Creation or new Production of <u>Righteousness</u> by the birth of the Spirit, besides his birth or Conception <u>Natural</u>, by which he becomes a <u>man</u>."[41] However, in the sixteenth and seventeenth centuries this recurrent rebirth metaphor was more than a commonplace, for Christians of the period believed that the State of Grace effected a complete transformation in the individual personality. St. Augustine in his <u>Confessions</u> had left his Renaissance readers a record and pattern of such regeneration within the human soul. Praising the Lord, he had exclaimed, "I will love thee, O Lord, and thank thee, and confess to thy name, because thou hast put away me such wicked and evil deeds. To thy grace I attribute it and to thy mercy, that thou hast melted away my sin as if it were ice."[42] And in the seventeenth century, an amazed John Bunyan overheard people discussing their conversion experiences, speaking of "a new birth," an alteration of consciousness which he at first could not comprehend: "their talk was about a new birth, the work of God on their hearts, also how they were convinced of their miserable state by nature; they talked how God had visited their souls with his love in the Lord Jesus, and with what words and promises they had been refreshed, comforted, and supported against the temptations of the devil. . . . they were to me as if they had found a new world."[43]

Regeneration, this spiritual transformation, was often portrayed in the imagery of nature in which the soul was a flower and grace the rebirth and renewal of all nature in springtime. This natural pattern of rebirth has, of course, been associated with religion since pagan fertility rites, and underlies much of the Christian symbolism for Easter. The religious poets of the seventeenth century drew upon this archetypal pattern as well, as they described the springtime of grace within their souls. George Herbert portrayed such a renewal in his poem "The Flower":

> How fresh, O Lord, how sweet and clean
> Are thy returns! ev'n as the flowers in spring,
> To which, besides their own demean,
> The late-past frosts tributes of pleasure bring.
> Grief melts away
> Like snow in May,
> As if there were no such cold thing.
> Who would have thought my shrivel'd heart
> Could have recovered greennesse?

(ll. 1-9)

In Henry Vaughan's "Unprofitableness," a poem obviously influenced by Herbert, one finds a similar use of natural imagery, interwoven with Christian double meanings:

How rich, O Lord! How fresh thy visits are!
'Twas but Just now my Bleak leaves hopeless hung
    Sullyed with dust and mud;
Each snarling blast shot through me, and did share
Their Youth, and beauty, cold showres nipt, and wrung
    Their spiciness, and blood;
But since thou didst in one sweet glance survey
Their sad decays, I flourish, and once more
    Breath all perfumes, and spice;
I smell a dew like Myrrh, and all the day
Wear in my bosome a full Sun.

                        (ll. 1-11)

In Vaughan's "The Morning-Watch," his soul breaks forth, again with nature imagery, in a dawn of sheer spiritual joy:

O Joyes! Infinite sweetnes! with what flowres;
And shoots of glory, my soul breakes, and buds!
        All the long houres
        Of night, and Rest
        Through the still shrouds
        Of sleep, and Clouds,
    This Dew fell on my Breast;
        O how it Blouds,
And Spirits all my Earth! heark! In what Rings,
And Hymning Circulation the quick world
        Awakes, and sings.

                        (ll. 1-11)

Another favorite means of portraying the magical transformation wrought by regeneration was the language of alchemy. For one thing, in the mélange of science and spiritual lore comprising alchemy, the "state of grace" was a synonym for the final step in transmutation, a process by which base metals were slowly purged, purified, and transformed into gold.[44] The spiritual analogy is obvious: a fallen soul, a "base metal," was, through the process of repentance and regeneration transformed into the "pure gold" of one redeemed in Christ. In Herbert's "The Elixer," the human heart is the base metal, and God the alchemist who transforms it with the "tincture" of grace to a philosopher's stone:

All may of thee partake:
Nothing can be so mean,
Which with his tincture (for thy sake)
    Will not grow bright and clean.
. . . .
This is the famous stone
That turneth all to gold:
For that which God doth touch and own
    Cannot for lesse be told.   (ll. 13-16; 21-24)

In "To all Angels and Saints" Herbert extended this analogy to Mary, the mother of Christ:

> Thou art the holy mine, whence came the gold,
> The great restorative for all decay
>   In young and old.

(ll. 11-13)

Here Christ himself is the gold which restores his people to eternal life. In "Easter" Herbert again celebrated the Redemption and the spiritual transmutation of grace within the human soul:

> Rise heart; thy Lord is risen. . . .
> That, as his death calcined thee to dust,
> His life may make thee gold, and much more, just.

(ll. 1-6)

John Donne expanded the grace/alchemy analogy in one of his sermons, describing the entire conversion process in alchemical terms. God, according to Donne:

> improves us, to a better condition, than we were in, at first. And this he does, first by purging and purifying us, and then by changing, and transmuting us. He purges us by his sunshine, by his temporal blessings; for, as the greatest globes lye nearest the face and top of the earth, where they have received the best concoction from the heat of the sun; so certainly, in reason; they who have Gods continual sun-shine upon them, in a prosperous fortune, should have received the best concoction, the best digestion of the testimonies of his love, and consequently be the purer, and the more refined metall, if this purging prevail not, then he comes to purge those whom he meanes to lay up in his treasure, with tribulation; he carries them from the sun-shine into the fire, and therefore, if those tribulations fall upon thee in a great and heavy measure, think thy dross needed this vehemence.[45]

Suffering, Donne acknowledged, was God's means of purging the dross from one's soul. In his divine poems, Donne, conscious of his sinfulness, called out to God to purify him in this manner. In one of the holy sonnets, he described himself as a little world, created by God, yet devastated by sin:

>   alas the fire
> Of lust and envie have burnt it heretofore,
> And made it fouler; Let their flames retire,
> And burne me ô Lord, with a fiery zeale

53

Of thee and thy house, which doth in eating heale.

("I am a little world made cunningly," ll. 10-14)

Again using alchemical allusions, he concluded "Goodfriday 1613. Riding Westward" with this colloquy, asking God to purge his soul and make him worthy:

> O Saviour, as thou hangs't upon the tree;
> I turne my backe to thee, but to receive
> Corrections, till thy mercies bid thee leave.
> O thinke mee worth thine anger, punish mee,
> Burne off my rusts, and my deformity,
> Restore thine Image, so much, by thy grace,
> That thou may'st know mee, and I'll turne my face.

(ll. 36-42)

Thomas Traherne also employed alchemical symbols to describe the workings of grace within the human heart. In this passage from <u>Meditations on the Six Days of the Creation</u> he called upon Jesus to "purify Man's heart, and mine in particular. O be unto me a refining Fire; sever the Dross from the Gold, that I may have no Dross left in me. Melt my Heart that it may vapour into Tears to thee, and that it may be softened and refined by thy Heat to praise thee."[46]

Associated with the magic of alchemy and the life-cycle of nature, the process of grace within the soul was, as we have seen, a topic of vital interest in the Renaissance. No less absorbing was the ultimate result of this transformation: one's condition in the State of Grace. Robert Rollock, like St. Augustine before him, maintained that the individual will was sanctified and strengthened by grace.[47] John Donne also attributed to regenerate individuals an increased joy and contentment: "for howsoever we cannot say that repentance is as happy an estate as Innocency, yet certainly every particular man feels more comfort and spiritual joy, after a true repentance for a sin, then he had in that degree of Innocency which he had before he committed that sinne."[48] Thomas Jackson associated regeneration with a sense of health and well-being: "an evidence of spiritual welfare or internall sense, directly answering to that naturall evidence or certaine knowledge men have of their health, or hearty cheerefulnesse, when their spirits are lively and their bodies strong, not disturbed with bad humours, their mindes not cumbred or disquieted with anxious carking thoughts."[49] And finally, according to Henry More, the regenerate were even transformed in appearance: "One may even in their Eyes and Aspects behold a Light and Comliness growing on."[50]

Regeneration, as Jacob Boehme and others have explained, was essentially an "unselfing," a release from the bondage of misery to an expansive new state of consciousness. Reborn in Christ, the individual became aware of his part in the divine plan. In Boehme's words, "He breaketh Self-hood, as a Vessel, wherein he lieth captive, and buddeth forth continually in Gods Will-spirit, with his Desire Resigned in God, (as a fair blossom springeth out of the Earth,) and worketh in and with God, what God pleaseth."[51] Henry Scougal, concurring with Boehme, maintained that for salvation "Self must be annihilated." One must transcend the limits of self as he is "translated from the First into the Second Adam."[52]

Ultimately, then, the State of Grace involved a movement from self-conscious limitation to a new degree of faith and oneness with God. As Louis Martz has recognized, the ultimate result of regeneration for the seventeenth century was the renewal of God's image in the human soul.[53] Thomas Jackson, speaking for his contemporaries, concluded that grace "consists in the assimilation or transformation of our spirit into the similitude or likeness of the spirit of God: and this is wrought by the renewing of God's image in us."[54]

Because Christians were able to attain a higher state of grace in the Redemption than had been known in Innocence, the Fall was considered, in retrospect, a felix culpa. "Now in Christ our redeemer, our estate is farre better, then even it was in Adam in his first creation," John Moore wrote in A Mappe of Mans Mortalitie.[55] And Milton explained in Areopagitica that the intuitive goodness of Adam in paradise was far surpassed by the mature faith of one who has known the conflict of good and evil, suffered temptation and yet persevered, for he is the "true wayfaring/warfaring Christian," the model for success in this world.[56]

As Milton and his contemporaries realized, the perfection of the individual's soul in Christ, begun in the State of Grace, is not completed until the State of Glory in the afterlife. Until then, people are still subject to their own human weaknesses and the vicissitudes of the world. For this reason, in the seventeenth century, the State of Grace was also known as the State of Trial, for souls are tried continually by the events of this life until their translation to eternal perfection. John Woolton explained how even after his conversion, one can experience spiritual setbacks and slip into sin, by his very nature as a fallible human being: "ignorances of God and spiritual thinges (not knowen unto us by nature) do oftentimes exceedingly encomber and unquiet even the man regenerate: So that light and darknes in mans minde, doo contende and strive one with another, as the Apostle most gravely teacheth in these wordes: The flesh coveteth against the spirite, and the spirite against the fleshe: these are contrarie one to another. And nowe and then the ignorance & darknes of the minde doth extinguish the small light kindled, eyther with grosse securitie, or curious philosophie, or carnall reason."[57] As Woolton noted, even "some excellent men, accompted lightes of the Church, doo often times erre & fall very grossely" because even they are subject to trial from two sources: "First the sicknes of originall sinne remayning yet in the posteritie of Adam: and secondly, the craft, furor, and power of the divell, who without gods especiall & wonderfull grace is able to do muche agaynst seely and weake men."[58]

Thus, all Christians are subject to a restless imperfection, even after their regeneration. This State of Trial, as George Herbert portrayed it, was essential to the human condition, even necessary to God's plan, to keep people ever striving for something beyond this world. As he explained in "The Pulley," the human estate is one of "repining restlessnesse" of which God has declared:

> Let him be rich and wearie, that at last,
> If goodnesse lead him not, yet wearinesse
> May tosse him to my breast.

(ll. 17-20)

And as Henry Vaughan portrayed it:

> Man is the shuttle, to whose winding quest
> And passage through these looms
> God order'd motion, but ordain'd no rest.

("Man," ll. 26-28)

Because of the restlessness they experienced in the State of Grace, both Herbert and Vaughan wrote many poems in which a weary, repentant soul cries out to God, followed by others in which the soul is renewed in grace. The internal structure of The Temple is a series of such trials and renewals and as such reflects the struggle of a "wayfaring Christian," whose soul repeats his conversion in many subordinate cycles of death and rebirth on his journey to glory and ultimate oneness with God.

NOTES

[1] A Godly and Learned Exposition of Christs Sermon on the Mount (London, 1611), p. 365.

[2] The Practical Christian (London, 1670), p. 91.

[3] The Principal Grounds of Christian Religion (London, 1625), p. 8.

[4] Pious Annotations Upon the Holy Bible (London, 1651), sig. A4.

[5] Bartlet, p. 155.

[6] Daniel Featly, Ancilla Pietatis: Or, the Hand-Maid to Private Devotion (London, 1616), pp. 11-12. See also Thomas Jackson, A Treatise of the Primaeval Estate of the First Man, in The Works of the Reverand and Learned Divine, Thomas Jackson, D.D. (London, 1673), III, 149 ff.

[7] Paradise Lost, II, 183-197, in The Works of John Milton, ed. Frank Allen Patterson et al. (New York: Columbia Univ. Press, 1931-1938), II. All quotations from Paradise Lost are from this text. See also Christian Doctrine, trans. John Carey, in Complete Prose Works of John Milton,

ed. Don M. Wolfe et al. (New Haven: Yale Univ. Press, 1973), VI, 448.

[8] Christian Ethicks (1675), ed. Carol L. Marks and George R. Guffey (Ithaca: Cornell Univ. Press, 1968), p. 74.

[9] The Guide Unto True Blessedness or, A Body of the Doctrine of the Scriptures, Directing man to the saving knowledge of God (London, 1625), pp. 32-33.

[10] Bartlet, p. 42.

[11] The City of God, trans. John Healey (London: J.M. Dent, 1940), p. 210.

[12] "Hymn to God my God, in my sicknesse," in The Poems of John Donne, ed. Herbert J.C. Grierson (Oxford, Oxford Univ. Press, 1912). All of Donne's poems cited here are from this edition. For a discussion of the iconographical background of this concept, see Rosamund Tuve, A Reading of George Herbert (London: Faber, 1951), pp. 82ff.

[13] "The Garden," in The Minor Poems of Joseph Beaumont, D.D. 1616-1699, ed. Eloise Robinson (Boston: Houghton Mifflin, 1914).

[14] A Treatise of the Primaeval Estate, p. 149.

[15] The Plaine Mans Path-way to Heaven (London, 1603), p. 7.

[16] A Double Catechisme (London, 1607), p. 15.

[17] Perkins, p. 24.

[18] Catholicism, for the most part, sees man's conversion to the State of Grace as a ritual repeated throughout the individual lifetime, not as the dramatic "conversion experience" described by the Protestants. In Catholic terms, the sinner is readmitted to God's grace through the Sacrament of Penance, a process "in which forgiveness of sins committed after baptism is granted through the priest's absolution to those who with true sorrow confess their sins and promise to satisfy for the same. . . . it comprises the actions of the penitent in presenting himself to the priest and accusing himself of his sins, and the actions of the priest in pronouncing absolution and imposing satisfaction. The whole process is called, from one of its parts, 'confession.'" (The Catholic Encyclopedia, ed. Charles G. Herbermann et al. (New York: Robert Appleton, 1907-1921), s.v. "Penance," XI, 618-19.) In addition, Catholics believe that "good works give an increase of grace," a point of disagreement with Luther and generations of Protestants (s.v. "Grace," in The Catholic Encyclopedia, VI, 709).

[19] A Briefe Method of Catechising (London, 1597), p. 27.

[20] Bartlet, p. 47.

[21]"Third Part of the Sermon of Salvation," in Certaine Sermons or Homilies Appointed to be Read in Churches in the Time of the Late Queen Elizabeth of Famous Memory and now thought fit to be reprinted by authority from the King's most excellent Majesty anno 1623 (Oxford: Oxford Univ. Press, 1844), p. 25.

[22]A Treatise of the Primaeval Estate, p. 149.

[23]The Fall of Man or the Corruption of Nature (London, 1616), p. 7.

[24]Bartlet, p. 164.

[25]Robert Rollock, A Treatise of Gods Effectual Calling, trans. Henry Holland (London, 1603), p. 127.

[26]The Righteous Mans Evidence for Heaven (London, 1624), p. 30.

[27]The Balm of Gilead (London, 1650), p. 94.

[28]In An Exposition upon the Epistle to the Colossians (London, 1617), Nicholas Byfield observed, "The degrees of grace in the third estate, are 1. vocation. 2. faith. 3. remission of sinnes. 4. sanctification of voca- tion" (sig. ¶3v); and Isaac Penington in Expositions with Observations Sometimes, on Several Scriptures, London, 1656, explained, "in this call there are four steps or degrees. First, The discovery of our present es- tate, which man never knoweth effectually till the time of his call. (It is the light of God alone which truly maketh darkness manifest.) It is impossible to see that which light alone discovers, without light. Second- ly, the discovery of another state, a different estate, a contrary estate. Thirdly, there is (which necessarily floweth from the former) a kindling of a desire in the soul after a change. And then lastly, there is an effec- tual invitation, an invitation as leaves no room for reluctancy or dispute, but forcibly carries the soul with it" (pp. 334-335).

[29]Rollock, p. 3.

[30]The Holy Pilgrime, Leading the way to New Jerusalem (London, 1609), pp. 216-17.

[31]Rollock, p. 127.

[32]Confessions, in Augustine: Confessions and Enchiridion, trans. Al- bert C. Outler (London: SCM Press, 1955), p. 144.

[33]Lever, p. 198.

[34]From Silex Scintillans (1655) in The Works of Henry Vaughan, ed. L.C. Martin (Oxford: Clarendon Press, 1957). All of Vaughan's poems cited are from this edition.

[35]Lever, p. 173.

[36]From The Temple in The Works of George Herbert, ed. F.E. Hutchinson (Oxford: Clarendon Press, 1941). All of Herbert's works cited are from this edition.

[37]Penington, p. 337.

[38]Bartlet, p. 155.

[39]A Newe Anatomie of whole man, aswell of his body, as of his Soule: Declaring the condition and constitution of the same, in his first creation, corruption, regeneration and glorification (London, 1576), sig. D4-D4v.

[40]Woolton, sig. D3v.

[41]A Treatise of the Primaeval Estate, p. 157.

[42]Confessions, p. 58.

[43]Grace Abounding to the Chief of Sinners (1666), (New York: Everyman's Library, 1928), p. 16.

[44]For a modern discussion of the language of alchemy, see Titus Burkhardt, Alchemy: Science of the Cosmos, Science of the Soul, trans. William Stoddart (Baltimore: Penguin Books, 1967), pp. 23 ff.

[45]"A Sermon Preached at Greenwich. April 30, 1615. Esay. 52.3.," in The Sermons of John Donne, ed. George R. Potter and Evelyn M. Simpson (Berkeley: University of California Press, 1953-1962), I, 163-64. All of Donne's sermons cited are from this edition.

[46]Meditations on the Six Days of the Creation (1717), intro. George Robert Guffey. Augustan Repr. Soc. Pub. No. 119 (Los Angeles: William Andrews Clark Memorial Library, 1966), p. 42. All citations are from this text.

[47]Augustine, "On Free Will," in Augustine: Earlier Writings, ed. John H.S. Burleigh (Philadelphia: Westminster Press, n.d.), p. 103; Rollock, p. 4.

[48]"Sermon Preached Feb 21 1618/19 on Matt. 21.44," in Sermons, II, 196.

[49]Justifying Faith (London, 1615), p. 24.

[50]Enchiridion Ethicum, the English translation of 1690 reproduced from the first edition (New York: Facsimile Text Society, 1930), p. 249.

[51] Jakob Behemen (Jacob Boehme), Signatura Rerum: or the Signature of all Things: Shewing the Sign, and Signification of the severall Forms and Shapes in the Creation, trans. J. Ellistone (London, 1651), p. 185.

[52] Vital Christianity: A Briefe Essay on the Life of God in the Soul of Man (London, 1725), p. 16.

[53] The Poetry of Meditation (New Haven: Yale Univ. Press, 1954), p. 150.

[54] A Treatise of the Primaeval Estate, p. 122.

[55] A Mappe of Mans Mortalitie, Clearely manifesting the originall of Death, with the Nature, Fruits, and Effects thereof, both to the Unregenerate, and Elect Children of God (London, 1617), pp. 82-83.

[56] Areopagitica, in Complete Works of John Milton, ed. Douglas Bush et al. (New Haven: Yale Univ. Press, 1959), II, 515.

[57] Woolton, sig. D7.

[58] Woolton, sig. D7.

Ens, tumidus, tenuis ; fulſi, cecidi, reſilivi ;
Dives, inops, ingens ; ſorte, dolore, fide.

The State of Glory

CHAPTER V

THE STATE OF GLORY

The Individual in Glory

The lifetime of individual Christians, their pilgrimage through the three earthly estates, leads ultimately to the State of Glory or Bliss. This is their raison d'être, their ultimate goal, according to Christian tradition. Only the State of Glory fully undoes the effects of the Fall and restores souls to their initial splendor as the image of God. In this fourth and final estate redeemed Christians manifest the glory of their creator and the miracle of the felix culpa, in which they are restored to a higher state than that from which they originally fell. Only in Glory is the cycle of creation complete and the circle made once again whole as the soul transfigured reflects the perfect love of its Creator.

Glory, signifying light, splendor, and honor, has long been associated with God. In Exodus we are told that "the glory of the LORD appeared in the cloude" (16:10), and "the glory of the LORD abode upon mount Sinai" (24:16). In the New Testament Christ manifests this glory. As John 1:14 states: "the Word was made flesh, and dwelt amongst us, (& we beheld his glory, the glory as of the onely begotten of the Father,) full of grace and truth."[1] Glory, then, is a manifestation of divinity. In a human soul it is a realization of the divine image inherent within its nature, in union and oneness with God. By the Redemption, fallen men and women were restored to the possibility of reflecting, more perfectly than ever before, the divinity with which humanity had been created. In John 17: 21-23 we are told that Christ prayed for mankind at Gesthemane, "that the world may beleeve that thou hast sent mee. And the glory which thou gavest me, I have given them: that they may be one, even as we are one: I in them, and thou in mee, that they may bee made perfect in one." God "called us to glory" in the Redemption, according to the Apostle Peter, that we "might bee partakers of the divine nature, having escaped the corruption that is in the world" (2 Peter 1:4).

To Renaissance commentators, the State of Glory for an individual meant the union of his soul with God in Heaven. As Paul Bayne explained in An Epitome of Mans Misery and Deliverie, "the estate which the godly shal enjoy after the labours of this life outwrastled, is called the state of glory, because the glory of God in the glorifying of his creature, shall bee particularly and especially revealed."[2] William Perkins, like Bayne, described for his followers the promised "kingdom of glorie,

. . . the blessed estate of all the Saints in Heaven."[3]

Free at last from all the corruption and mutability of this world, the individual soul in the State of Glory will experience joy and life everlasting. Henry Vaughan explained in his translation of Anselmus's Man in Glory that the rewards of the faithful include "everlasting life, eternal happinesse, never-ending pleasures, and a fulness and sufficiency of all accommodations to their own desires without any scarcity, or want at all."[4] This expansive joy begins immediately after death, as John Bartlet affirmed: "As soon as the Soul is separated from the Body, it goes to the Spirit of just men made perfect, Heb. 12. It is perfected in all its Faculties, Understanding, Will, Memory, Affections."[5] The anticipation of such bliss was enough to send Henry More into ecstasies as he described the soul's entry into the State of Glory: "O the Joys! O the Triumphs! O what Embraces from that Illustrious Assembly! What Words, and Welcome, and Elogies will they bestow, for what she so direfully suffer'd, and so bravely overcame, in the defence of Virtue and of Truth! How will the Mansions above Eccho and Rebound, with Hallelujahs of that Heavenly quire! Or how rather, will this victorious Soul, enter with Triumph into those Mansions, where Felicity is never to end!"[6]

The State of Glory Beyond Time

Like the other three estates, the State of Glory was seen on both an individual and a historical level. Individually, as we have seen, all just souls were believed to enter Glory after death. However, according to the Bible and tradition, Glory in its historical dimensions will not transpire until the Second Coming, the Resurrection of the Dead, and the Last Judgment, when the redeemed are to be glorified in both body and soul; as it is written in Colossians 3:4, "When Christ, who is our life, shall appeare, then shall yee also appeare with him in glorie." Thus, St. Augustine conceived of the State of Glory as both individual and historical, existing "beyond this life in the repose of the spirit, and, at the last, in the resurrection of the body."[7] So also the prefatory poem attached to Donne's Second Anniversary depicts the soul of Elizabeth Drury as reposing in the individual State of Glory and anticipating a further consummation of Glory at the Last Judgment:

> Thy Soule (deare virgin) whose tribute is,
> Mov'd from this mortall Spheare to lively blisse;
> And yet moves still, and still aspires to see
> The worlds last day, thy glories full degree.

(ll. 3-6)[8]

The historical state of Glory, as Nicholas Byfield explained, consisted of "Three things, the Resurrection from the dead, the last Judgement, and the Glory of Heaven."[9] The first of these, the Resurrection of the dead, was a subject of meditation for many, including, characteristically, John Donne, who explored it in this passage from one of his sermons:

Where be all the Atoms of that flesh, which a <u>Corrasive</u>
hath eat away, or a <u>Consumption</u> hath breath'd, and ex-
hal'd away from our arms, and other Limbs? In what
wrinkle, in what furrow, in what bowel of the earth, ly
all the graines of the ashes of a body burnt a thousand
years since? In what corner, in what ventricle of the
sea, lies all the jelly of a Body drowned in the <u>generall</u>
<u>flood</u>? What cohaerence, what sympathy, what depen-
dence maintaines any relation, any correspondence, between that arm that was lost in Europe, and that legge
that was lost in Afrique or Asia, scores of years between?
One humour of our dead body produces worms, and those
worms suck and exhaust all other humour, and then all
dies, and all dries, and molders into dust, and that dust
is blowed into the River, and that puddled water tumbled
into the sea, and that ebs and flows in infinite revolutions,
and still, God knows in what <u>Cabinet</u> every <u>seed-Pearle</u>
lies, in what part of the world every graine of every mans
dust lies; and <u>sibilat populum suum</u>, (as his Prophet speaks
in another case) he whispers, he hisses, and he beckons
for the bodies of his Saints, and in the twinckling of an
eye, that body that was scattered over all the elements,
is sate down at the right hand of God, in a glorious
resurection.[10]

Unlike Donne, who emphasized the miracle of the resurrection by
dwelling on the corruption wrought by death, George Herbert portrayed
the resurrection from a different point of view. His poem "Dooms-day"
depicts a wondrous and joyous awakening:

> Come away,
> Make no delay.
> Summon all the dust to rise,
> Till it stirre, and rubbe the eyes;
> While this member jogs the other,
> Each one whispring, <u>Live you brother</u>?
> . . . .
> Come away,
> Thy flock doth stray.
> Some to windes their bodie lend,
> And in them may drown a friend:
> Some in noisome vapours grow
> To a plague and publick wo.
> Come away.
> Help our decay.
> Man is out of order hurl'd,
> Parcel'd out to all the world,
> Lord, thy broken consort raise,
> And the musick shall be praise.

(ll. 1-6, 19-30)[11]

65

Many theologians and laymen in this period believed that the biblical prophecies of Glory in Matthew 16:27 would shortly come to pass, that "the Sonne of man" would soon "come in the glory of his Father, with his Angels: and . . . reward every man according to his workes." According to a modern historian, "the tension produced by the Reformation . . . combined with nationalism, Protestant literalism, Calvinist elitism and perhaps Lollard tradition to produce widespread apocalyptic and and millenarian beliefs" in sixteenth- and seventeenth-century England.[12] Commentators, astrologers and numerologists predicted that the Second Coming was very nearly at hand. Joseph Mede declared that the period of the forty-two months mentioned in the book of Revelations would end some time "between the yeers 1625 and 1715," placing the Apocalypse in or near the seventeenth century.[13] Henry Archer, in The Personall Reign of Christ upon Earth (1642), predicted the end of the world in the year 1666,[14] and three years later Christian astrologer William Lilly concurred with this prediction, relating these old English prophecies to his own astrological projections:

> Remember M.D.C.L.X.
> V. and I. then nere a Rex.
> Observe, quoth [the ancient prophet], if there be ever
> a King in England, in the year 1666. nay he positively
> maintaines the contrary: The Stars tell also of a great
> change in this Kingdome somewhat before.
> Mark the holy written Beast,
> Six hundred sixty six, it heast.
> An allusion to the number, signifying Antichrist, and
> intimates no more than the wonderfulnesse of those yeer,
> or times about 1666. and this not improbably, the influence and efficacy of the third Conjunction of Saturne
> and Jupiter, in Sagitarrius then impending, which I am
> assured will produce no small alteration in the Church
> and Common-wealth of England.[15]

With predictions like this in their minds, many Englishmen in the second quarter of the seventeenth century began to interpret political and astrological phenomena as religious signs or mysteries. William Lilly had written that "many high mysteries concerning the full and perfect understanding of . . . our Saviour Jesus Christ, and many places of Scripture not hitherto rightly explained, shall now . . . by some new enlightened holy men, into whom God shall poure a more full and cleerer understanding, be thoroughly revealed, even to the meaning of the easiest capacity."[16] And many, indeed, believed themselves prophets of a new age. In his New Atlantis and plans for the Great Instauration Sir Francis Bacon revealed his belief that with the new science people could improve their fallen estate and inaugurate a millenium of progress.[17] John Milton believed for a time that the political reforms of the Puritans could bring about the Millenium. "This great and warlike Nation," he wrote in Of Reformation (1611),

> instructed and inur'd to the fervent and continuall practice

of Truth and Righteousnesse, and casting farre from her
the rags of her old vices may press on hard to that high
and happy emulation to be found the soberest, wisest, and
most Christian People at that day when thou the Eternall
and shortly-expected King shall open the Clouds to judge
the severall Kingdomes of the World, and distributing
Nationall Honours and Rewards to Righteous and just Com-
monwealths, shalt put an End to all Earthly Tyrannies,
proclaiming thy universal and milde Monarchy through
Heaven and Earth.[18]

In addition to such important figures as Bacon and Milton, others of less
importance regarded themselves as the "new enlightened holy men" of
whom Lilly had written. As a modern scholar points out,

In 1644 . . . a labourer named Rowland Bateman claimed to
be both the Son of God and Abraham [and in spite of the
confusion of his ideas he had quite a large following.] He
announced that he must be hanged, and would rise again
on the third day, and that the millenium would begin in
nine years' time. . . . Rhys or 'Arise' Evans, a Welsh tail-
or, stood up in St. Botolph's, Bishopsgate, in 1647 and
proclaimed that he was Christ. . . . Several women claimed
to be with child by the Holy Ghost, and that their child
would be the Messiah.[19]

The Civil War, breaking out in 1642, was seen by many as "the deci-
sive apocalyptic or millenarian struggle."[20] The court of Charles I with
his French Catholic Queen, Henrietta Maria, and the high Anglican nature
of the Laudian Church "made it easy [for many] to identify the royalist
cause with the Papal Antichrist."[21] The fall of the royalist cause represented to militant Protestants the fall of Babylon, and they waited an-
xiously for the New Jerusalem and the establishment of the Kingdom of
God on Earth. In the forefront of this movement were the violent Fifth
Monarchy Men, who advocated the destruction by force of all government
and the inversion of the established social order to prepare the world for
the reign of King Jesus. Not satisfied even with the Puritan common-
wealth, they persisted in stirring up discord, long after the revolution was
past.[22]

Biblical tradition maintains that the world at the Second Coming
will be destroyed by fire. 2 Peter 3:12, one of many eschatological passages in the Bible, described "the comming of the day of God, wherein
the heavens being on fire shall be dissolved, and the Elements shall melt
with fervent heat." Many commentators, among them Martin Luther,
likened this final conflagration to alchemical purification. According to
Luther,

as in a furnace the fire extracts and separates from a substance the other portions, and carries upward the spirit, the
life, the sap, the strength, while the unclean matter, the

dregs, remain at the bottom, like a dead and worthless car-
cass; even so God, at the day of judgement, will separate
all things through fire, the righteous from the ungodly. The
Christians and righteous shall ascend upward into heaven,
and there live everlastingly, but the wicked and ungodly, as
the dross and filth, shall remain in hell, and there be damned.[23]

Joseph Mede also emphasized this "destruction . . . by fire; whereby the
world shall be purified as gold, and shall be freed from the servitude of
the curse, under which it groaneth by reason of mans sinne into the glorious libertie of the sonnes of God."[24] Is it any wonder, then, that in the
year 1666, a year in which the English were ravaged by "War, a consuming
Pestilence, and a more consuming Fire,"[25] there was again a general un-
rest as individuals thought back upon early prophecies and the plagues and
fire described in the Book of Revelations? The sight of London consumed
by flames that seemed to reach up to the very heavens, and stricken by a
plague in which hundreds of bodies at a time were carted off to common
graves must have brought terror to the hearts of men and women. Anticipating the Last Judgment at any moment, they must have felt, as in
Revelations 6:17, that "the great day of his wrath was come," and that
they, like St. John the Divine, were shortly to see

> a great white throne, and him that sate on it, from whose
> face the earth and the heaven [would flee] away, and there
> [would be] found no place for them.
> 12 And . . . the dead, small and great, [would] stand before
> God: and the books [would be] opened: & another booke
> [would be] opened, which is the booke of life: and the dead
> [would be] judged out of those things which [are] written
> in the books, according to their works.

(Rev. 20:11-12)

To return from the historical ramifications of the State of Glory to
the tradition itself, following the Resurrection of the Dead and the Last
Judgment, there will be established, according to the Bible, "a new heav-
en, and a new earth" (Rev. 21:1): the old world destroyed by fire to make
way for the new. The redeemed souls shall then enter the New Jerusalem,
a city of infinite beauty, where they shall live for all eternity. This city,
seen in a prophetic vision by St. John, is described in luminous terms in
Revelations. Made of "pure gold, like unto cleare glasse" and glowing
with emeralds, saphires, and pearls, the heavenly city will be a city of
light, even as God is light (21:18-21). According to Rev. 21:23 "the citie
had no need of the Sunne, neither of the Moone to shine in it. for the
glory of God did lighten it." This "Glorious place" or "highest Heaven"
John Bartlet has described, again in terms of light: "wholly Light, not only bespangled here and there with glittering Stars, but as one great Sun,
and that which is increased by the admirable splendor of the glorified
Body of Jesus Christ, and those millions of glorified Saints, whose Bodies
there shall shine, not onely as the Stars, Dan. 12 but as the Sun, Mat.
13.43."[26]

68

In this resplendent Heaven will dwell the glorified bodies and souls of redeemed Christians forevermore. But what, according to tradition, will this glorified condition entail? Some commentators felt that a vision of such ecstatic perfection simply could not be grasped by the limited minds of this world. According to John Bartlet, "the happy estate of Man by Glorification . . . Eternal Glory, Is that which God will confer upon the Saints in Heaven: If you ask what that is? We must answer in the words of Austin, Facilius est excogitare, quid non fit, quam quid fit: It cannot be conceived, much less expressed."[27] Anselmus, however, attempted to convey to mortal minds a glimpse of the total fulfillment possible in the State of Glory. "What dost thou thinke then will thy condition be," he asked, "when thou shalt eternally injoy all these things; namely, Beauty, Strength, Swiftnesse of motion, Liberty, Health, Pleasure, Length of Life, Wisedome, Love, Peace, Power, Honour, and a Security of all."[28]

Physically glorified, individuals in this most perfect state will radiate beauty and light, according to John Woolton: "Shining brightnes is . . . . ascribed by the schoole men to glorified bodyes: wherof the Apostle speaketh thus: Christ shall chaunge our vile bodies, and make them like to his glorious body, &c. Some signe & token hereof was given by Christ in hys transfiguration, when his face did shine like the sun: & the Evangelist saith: The just shall shine as the sunne in the sight of God."[29] Anselmus added that "in the life to come the beauty of the righteous shall shine equally with the Sunne, . . . the body of our Lord Jesus Christ . . . shall outshine the brightnesse of the Sun. But by the testimony of the Apostle we shall be made like unto him. for he saith, He shall change our vile bodies, that they may be fashioned like unto his glorious body."[30] Anselmus also stated that in Glory mankind will radiate perfect health: the "health of the life to come shall fill the whole man with such an immutable, inviolable, and inexpressable sweetnesse and solace, as shall utterly repel and for ever drive away all thoughts of infirmities, their accessions, or revolutions."[31] Another interesting speculation about the human body in the state of Glory is Gervase Babington's reference to the "fantasticall Anabaptists, that will goe naked" to declare their belief that their lost innocence is "regayned in measure by Christ, and shall presently be injoyed in the life to come, when nakednesse shall shame us no more then it did at the first."[32]

Men and women in this state will have their bodies glorified beyond all human limitations. Anselmus even believed that glorification would give people the strength of supermen: "the Citizens of the new Jerusalem shall excell so much in strength, that nothing can have power to resist them: whether their desire be to remove, or over-turn any thing out of its station, or by any other way to divert it, nothing can hinder them; nor shall they in compassing their desire be put to any more trouble or pains, then we are put to at present when we move an Eye, or turne it towards any object we desire to look upon."[33]

In addition to their strength, which will enable them to accomplish all they desire, glorified humans will, again according to Anselmus, possess the speed and agility of angels. "As for Activity," he explained, "we shall be indued with such a measure of it, as shall render us equall for swiftnesse to the very Angels of God, which in a moment passe from the highest heaven unto the earth, and from the earth again into heaven."[34]

As for our perceptive powers in the State of Glory, one need only refer to 1 Cor. 13:12: "now we see through a glasse, darkely: but then face to face: now I know in part; but then I shall know even as I am knowen." Our vision, dark and limited in this mortal state, will in Glory be direct, unimpaired, and intuitive, allowing the glorified to perceive God and one another "face to face." As John Donne explained in one of his sermons, "how highly soever the body of the Father, or of my friend shall be glorifyed there, mine eyes shall be glorified as much, and we are both kept in the same proportion there, as wee had towards one another here; . . . . I shall not know my selfe, nor that state of glory which I am then in, by any light of Nature which, brought thither, but by that light of Glory which I shall receive there."[35] Moreover, "our wisdome," as Anselmus revealed, "shall be so great in the life to come, that nothing shall be hidden from us, that we have a minde to knowe; for we shall know all things; which God ordained to be known of man, as well those things which are past, as those which (in this world) are yet to come. There all men shall be known by every man, and every man shall be known by all men."[36]

In addition to this increased wisdom and powers of perception, one's will will be strengthened unalterably in the direction of good. As William Perkins explained, in "The last estate . . . the estate of glorification after this life. . . . the libertie of will is certen freedome, onely to will that which is good, and pleasing unto God. For it is the continual voice (as it were) and crie of the glorified will: I doe no evill, and I will not doe it: I doe that which is good, and I will doe it. And this indeede is the perfecte libertie, in which mans will is conformed to the Free-will of God and good Angels who will onely that which is good, and cannot will that which is evill."[37] To the postlapsarian mind, this description of the glorified will seems strangely at variance with our notions of free will. However, perhaps a passage from one of Donne's sermons helps clarify this point. Donne believed that "he is admitted to [the] sight of God, can never look off, nor lose that sight againe. Only in heaven shall God proceed to this patefaction, this manifestation, this revelation of himself: And that by the light of glory."[38] To a glorified soul in full communion with God, then, there will simply be no alternative to the total perception of good, and evil, as such, will cease to exist.

John Woolton wondered "whether, in the state of glorification men shall knowe such as were their acquaintance & frends in this life."[39] And among the other religious writers of the period, the answer, or at least the expectation, seems to have been universally "yes." Donne, in his commemorative sermon on the death of Magdalen Herbert Danvers, certainly looked for the reunion of divided families and friends on the last day: "and though [God divides] man and wife, mother and child, friend

70

and friend, by the hand of Death, [he does so] with this consolation, that though we part at divers daies, and by divers waies, here, yet wee shall all meet at one place, and at one day, a day that no night shall determine, the day of the glorious Resurrection."[40] Anselmus, also, saw the reunion of loved ones, the communion of saints, as one of the prime joys of the State of Glory. There, he felt, would be "a certaine inestimable and inviolable friendship. . . . which shall so warm the hearts of every one towards another, that the love which every one shall have for another, shall be evident and convincing in the knowledge of all."[41] One's own happiness will be multiplied by witnessing the happiness of his friends, he explained, "For if thou hadst any Friend, whom thou didst love as well as thy selfe, and in whose good thou wouldst rejoyce as in thy owne, and shouldst see this friend admitted to the same Heaven, and happinesse with thy selfe; wouldst thou not extremely rejoyce in his Felicity? But if thou hadst two or three, or more such friends, and shouldest see them all glorified with a state equal to thy own, would not thy joyes also exceed, and increase together with their number?"[42] In "this perfect friendship in the state of glory," Anselmus could conceive of no disagreement, no note of discord in any relationship. Here, he felt, would be such oneness, "such perfect agreement and unity there betwixt all, that none shall dissent from that which another desires."[43]

As John Bartlet has pointed out, in the State of Glory one will not only enjoy the company of friends he knew while on earth, but the "communion of saints," uniting the faithful from the beginning to the end of time. "There," according to Bartlet, "you shall have the society not only of all your Christian Alliance, Friends and Acquaintance, that have liv'd and dyed in the Lord, but of all the Holy Patriarchs, Prophets, Apostles, Martyrs, Saints; not only of the Glorious Angels, but the ever blessed Trinity."[44]

Communication was believed to be improved and refined in the State of Glory. According to Godfrey Goodman, because our bodies "shall be much more spirituall, and [our] understanding more illuminated, then ever before; . . . we shall then be like the Angels of heaven, who speake to each other by directing the edge of their understanding to each other as it were opening the glasses, and casting forth a light to each other."[45] In Glory we will communicate more clearly, more directly, with something resembling telepathy, for as Henry More maintained: "Holy Angels, and all those Resplendent Beings, which are above, do not onely behold the Beauties of each other, but Communicate, and even Discourse, by some unspeakable Way."[46]

Their bodies and souls glorified, and encompassed by the radiant multitude of all the redeemed saints, individuals in Glory will be blessed by a state of "perfect love & no feare."[47] Their joy will be boundless, their contentment complete, as John Donne proclaimed in one of his sermons: "Joy in a continuall dilation of thy heart, to receive augmentation of that which is infinite, in the accumulation of essential and accidentall joy. Joy in a continuall melting of indissoluble bowels, in joyfull and yet compassionate beholding thy Saviour."[48] Filled with divine love, the saints will rejoice exceedingly for all time. As Anselmus explained, they will "infinitly triumph in his Glory, and in his wonderful and inexpressible Joyes. They have Joy therefore within, and Joy without: Joy from above, and Joy beneath: In the Compasse, and Circuit of them there is Joy, and in a word every where."[49] "The fulnesse of those joyes breeds no surfeit," he explained. For "such delights as these are, . . . no man ever in this world did so far perceive or taste." Heavenly joys, far superior to the fleeting pleasures we know in this life, will bring a never-ending state of bliss to the redeemed. Infinite as well as eternal, these "ineffable and endlesse pleasures [shall] be poured upon, and over-flow the righteous [so that] their eyes, their eares, and their hearts, yea their very bones (as the Prophet David saith) shall be glad and rejoyce: every part and every member of them shall be crowned and replenished with the fulnesse and the life of pleasures."[50]

In the State of Glory, redeemed mankind shall wear for all eternity "a crowne of glory that fadeth not away" (1 Peter 5:4). As Woolton explained, "The state of man glorified excelleth the firste state of man after his creation" because the State of Glory "shal be perpetuall & unchangeable, whereas in the first state of man it was changeable, & indured for a short time."[51] The Redeemed shall experience a fulness of joy and security heretofore unknown to them. Unthreatened by change and mutability, they will know "a perpetuall security," realizing, according to Anselmus, that for all their lives "no accident whatsoever could rob [them] of [their] happinesse."[52] Henry More agreed that there one will find "no Vicissitudes; all is Peace, all Security, and all things are Stationary and fix'd. In short here is a Consummation of the Soul's blessed Estate."[53]

Glory, then is a completion, a consummation; it is the human soul at its most perfect, as the true reflection of its creator. In Glory, John Donne maintained, "We shall have this Image of God in Perfection."[54] There, Daniel Rogers explained, "shall bee a filing up of the soule with the perfect Image of God in light and Holines: and that by sight of the Glorified sence, beholding God as he is, and wholy transformed by the Mirror of his Majesty to Glory, so farre as our soule and body are capable of to the uttermost."[55]

In the State of Glory the individual and historical estates will merge forever in a perfection beyond time and the confines of this mutable world, generating a renewal, on a higher level, of the paradise of Eden and our original condition as children of God. In this fourth and final estate the progress of the soul will be concluded as in one sense the end of time returns us to the beginning, where man and woman are once again created in the image of God, this time more glorious than before. And the cycle of history, for the individual and mankind, will merge with what Thomas Traherne described as the "Infinit and Eternal Love" of the Creator who declared himself "Alpha and Omega, the beginning and the ending . . . , which is, and which was, and which is to come."[56]

NOTES

[1] The Holy Bible, Conteyning the Old Testament, and the new: New-ly Translated out of the Originall Tongues, & with the former Translations diligently compared and revised by his Majesties speciall Commandement. Appointed to be read in Churches (London, 1611). All biblical quotations are taken from this edition.

[2] An Epitome of Mans Misery and Deliverie (London, 1619), p. 3.

[3] A Godly and Learned Exposition of Christs Sermon on the Mount (London, 1611), p. 79.

[4] In The Works of Henry Vaughan, ed. L.C. Martin (Oxford: Clarendon Press, 1957), p. 194. All references to Anselmus are from this work.

[5] The Practical Christian (London, 1670), p. 167.

[6] Enchiridion Ethicum, the English translation of 1690 reproduced from the first edition (New York: Facsimile Text Society, 1930), p. 265.

[7] In Augustine: Confessions and Enchiridion, trans. Albert C. Outler (London: SCM Press, 1955), p. 410.

[8] "The Harbinger to the Progresse" in The Poems of John Donne, ed. Herbert J.C. Grierson (Oxford: Oxford Univ. Press, 1912), I, 249.

[9] The Principall Grounds of Christian Religion (London, 1625) p. 20.

[10] "A Sermon Preached at the Earl of Bridgewaters house in London at the mariage of his daughter, the Lady Mary, to the eldest sonne of the Lord Herbert of Castle-iland, Novemb. 19.1627. on Matth. 22.30," in The Sermons of John Donne, ed. George R. Potter and Evelyn Simpson (Berke-ley: University of California Press, 1953-1962), VIII, 98. All of Donne's sermons cited are from this edition.

[11] From The Temple in The Works of George Herbert, ed. F.E. Hutchinson (Oxford: Clarendon Press, 1941), pp. 186-87.

[12] B.S. Capp, The Fifth Monarchy Men: A Study in Seventeenth-cen-tury English Millenarianism (London: Faber, 1972), p. 35.

[13] "Discourse of the beginning and ending of the 42 moneths, or 1260 daies, Rev. 11." in Diatribae, p. 448.

[14] The Personall Reign of Christ Upon Earth (London, 1642), p. 46.

[15] A Collection of Ancient and Modern Prophesies (London, 1645), pp. 14-15.

[16] Lilly, p. 15.

[17] According to Benjamin Farrington, in Francis Bacon: Philosopher of Industrial Science (London: Lawrence and Wishart, 1951), p. 146, Bacon "had his share of the conviction, founded on the Bible, that he was the chosen instrument of God to work this great reform." See pp. 74-76 and 144-150 for a discussion of Bacon's vision of a coalescence of science and religion to produce an "ascent to glory" in this world (p. 150).

[18] Of Reformation in England in Complete Prose Works of John Milton, ed. Don M. Wolfe et al. (New Haven: Yale Univ. Press, 1953-1971), I, 616.

[19] Capp, p. 42.

[20] Capp, p. 35.

[21] Capp, p. 229.

[22] For further discussion, see Capp, p. 131 ff. and Ernest Lee Tuveson, Millennium and Utopia: A Study in the Background of the Idea of Progress (Berkeley: University of California Press, 1949), pp. 88-89.

[23] Table Talk in A Compend of Luther's Theology, ed. Hugh Thomson Kerr, Jr. (Philadelphia: Westminster Press, 1943), pp. 237-38.

[24] The Key of the Revelation, trans. Richard More (London, 1643), p. 129.

[25] From John Dryden's Preface to Annus Mirabilis; see The Works of John Dryden, ed. Edward Niles Hooker and H.T. Swedenberg, Jr. (Berkeley: University of California Press, 1956-19--), I, 48 and 258n.

[26] Bartlet, pp. 166-67.

[27] Bartlet, pp. 165-66.

[28] Anselmus, p. 208.

[29] A Newe Anatomie of whole man, aswell of his body, as of his Soule (London, 1576), sigs. F2v-F3.

[30] Anselmus, p. 195.

[31] Anselmus, p. 199.

[32] Certaine Plaine, briefe, and comfortable Notes, upon every Chapter of Genesis (London, 1596), p. 27.

[33] Anselmus, pp. 196-97.

[34] Anselmus, pp. 196-97.

[35]"Sermon Preached at Lincoln's Inne on 1 Cor. 15:50," in Sermons, III, 119.

[36]Anselmus, p. 201.

[37]A Treatise of God's Free Grace, & Man's Free-Will, in The Works of that famous and worthie Minister of Christ (London, 1612), I, 739.

[38]"Sermon Preached at S. Pauls, for Easter-day 1623 on 1 Cor. 13:12," in Sermons, VIII, 232.

[39]Sig. F8v.

[40]Prayer before the "Sermon of Commemoration of the Lady Danvers, late Wife of Sir John Danvers, on 2 Pet. 3:13, 1 July 1627," in Sermons, VIII, 62.

[41]Anselmus, p. 204.

[42]Anselmus, p. 205. Anselmus fails to mention whether the reverse of this is true, whether one's happiness in Glory is diminished by an awareness of some loved ones who were not admitted to Heaven.

[43]Anselmus, p. 205.

[44]Bartlet, pp. 166-67.

[45]The Fall of Man or the Corruption of Nature (London, 1616), II, 304.

[46]More, p. 265.

[47]Woolton, sig. G4.

[48]"Sermon Preached upon Whitsunday. At St. Pauls, 1622, on Rom. 8.16," in Sermons, V, 75.

[49]Anselmus, pp. 208-09.

[50]Anselmus, pp. 199-200.

[51]Woolton, sig. G1v.

[52]Anselmus, p. 207.

[53]More, p. 266.

[54]"Sermon Preached to the King, at the Court, Second Sermon on Gen. 1:26," in Sermons, IX, 89.

[55] A Practicall Catechisme (London, 1632), p. 218.

[56] Centuries of Meditations, in Centuries, Poems and Thanksgivings, ed. H.M. Margoliouth (Oxford: Clarendon Press, 1958), I (C IV: 72). Traherne paraphrases this quotation from Rev. 1:8.

CHAPTER VI

THOMAS TRAHERNE:
THE FOUR ESTATES AND INDIVIDUAL
DEVELOPMENT

Thomas Traherne's "Gospel of Felicity" was structured by the concept of the four estates. In his Centuries he encouraged his readers to meditate on this pattern: "to Contemplate GOD . . . in His Works of Providence. And Man, as he is a Creature of GOD, capable of Celestial Blessednesse, and a Subject in His Kingdom, in his four-fold Estate of Innocency, Misery, Grace, and Glory" (C III:43). The four estates represented for Traherne a progression within the consciousness of every redeemed individual. Moreover, Traherne documented this progression, repeatedly describing his own perceptions in the states of Innocence, Misery, and Grace, and looking ahead tohis hopes of Glory in the afterlife.

In his poetry as well as his prose, he portrayed these estates as stages in the evolution of consciousness, as the individual recapitulates in his own lifetime the Fall and Redemption,and is transformed by his conversion from the first to the second Adam. Traherne's poem "The Approach," for example, depicts his progression from Innocence, when God "in our Childhood with us walks/And with our Thoughts mysteriously He talks" to the alienation of Misery when "I careless was, nor did regard/ The End for which he all those Thoughts prepard," to his conversion when "Now, with new and open Eys,/ I see beneath, as if I were abov the Skies." In addition, Christian Ethicks, his guide for human conduct, is structured around "What Vertues belong to the Estate of Innocency, what to the Estate of Misery and Grace, and what to the Estate of Glory." In order to understand all that these estates represented for Traherne as they recurred throughout his works, let us consider them individually, beginning with the State of Innocence.

Innocence

Like many of his contemporaries, Traherne was fascinated by the State of Innocence, describing Adam's state before the Fall with obvious delight in his Centuries and Meditations on the Six Days of the Creation. His poem "Adam" gives us further insight into his opinions on the subject. Including all the usual elements: Adam's perfection in mind and body, his primitivism, his perfect contentment, this poem also illustrates Traherne's own preoccupation with perception. According to Traherne, the raison d'être for Adam and all his descendents was to reflect the glory and be-nevolence of their creator by enjoying the world set before them, mirror-ing its beauty in their minds and their thanksgivings. Naturally, Traherne felt that in order to be properly thankful for his state, one must appre-hend it fully. Thus, for Traherne, the greatest treasure in the State of Innocence was Adam's unfallen perception, his ability to see and know his divine inheritance: "The sense of what he did possess/ [which] Fill'd him with Joy and Thankfulness" ("Adam," 11.37-38).

Traherne believed that Adam's perception of unity and beauty in himself and his world was to some extent recapitulated in the conscious-ness of every child. More than a familiar metaphor, childhood innocence was for Traherne an epistemological reality, an insight into the workings of the human mind. As Stanley Stewart has noted, Traherne was unusual, even in an age so rich in gifted minds, for he anticipated theories devel-oped centuries later by Blake, Wordsworth, Thoreau, and Freud.[4]

Drawing upon memory and introspection, Traherne described the pri-mitivism experienced by children in the State of Innocence with references to his own childhood. For example, in "The Apostacy," he recalled how

> I did believ
> My self in Eden set
> Affecting neither Gold, nor Ermin'd Crowns,
> Nor ought els that I need forget.

(ll. 20-24)

Like Adam and Eve, he found his world simple, natural, and abundant, un-limited by notions of private property and materialism. "The State of In-nocence/ and Bliss," he asserted, "not Trades and Poverties,/ Did fill my Sence," ("Wonder," ll. 30-32). Unaware of private ownership, the child is therefore unaware of poverty, perceiving everything as his to enjoy:

> Proprieties themselvs were mine,
>   And Hedges Ornaments:
> Walls, Boxes, Coffers, and their rich Contents
>   Did not Divide my Joys, but shine
> Clothes, Ribbans, Jewels, Laces, I esteemd
>   My Joys by others worn;
> For me they all to wear them seemd
>   When I was born.

("Wonder," ll. 57-64)

Unconfused by the superficial values of the civilized world, the child, Tra-herne concluded, experiences an inner contentment not unlike that of Ad-am before the Fall. As he affirmed in the Centuries: "Certainly Adam in Paradice had not more Sweet and Curious Apprehensions of the World, than I when I was a child" (C III:1).

Traherne believed children were not only unaware of material concerns, but also unaware, and consequently innocent, of sin and corruption in the world and within themselves. Looking back on his own childhood in the poem "Innocence," he explained:

No inward Inclination did I feel
To Avarice or Pride: My Soul did kneel
In Admiration all the Day. No Lust, nor Strife,
    Polluted then my Infant Life.

No Fraud nor Anger in me movd
No Malice Jealousie or Spite;
All that I saw I truly lovd.
Contentment only and Delight
Were in my Soul.

(ll. 25-33)

Free from conflicts of motivation and perturbations of spirit, the child experiences an edenic contentment and inner peace; as Traherne affirmed in the same poem, in his childhood he

felt no Stain, nor Spot of Sin
No Darkness then did overshade,
But all within was Pure and Bright,
No Guilt did Crush, nor fear invade
But all my Soul was full of Light.

(ll. 4-8)

As some critics have pointed out, observations like these, seemingly at variance with the doctrine of original Sin, could have placed Traherne in a precarious theological position. However, Traherne's feelings about the State of Innocence, although paradoxical, were not heretical, but fell well within the bounds of seventeenth-century Anglicanism.[5] He subscribed to the orthodox doctrine of the Fall and original sin, yet at the same time he recalled experiencing a state of harmony that would, if taken literally, seem to belie this. As he declared in the Centuries, in his childhood, "I seemed as one brought into the Estate of Innocence" (C III:2), (italics mine). The child's perception of innocence, although from the theological standpoint an illusion, was psychologically a reality to Traherne. As Stanley Stewart has shown, the "sweet Mistake" in the perception of "unexperienc'd Infancy," the "Seeming somwhat more than View" that Traherne depicted in "Shadows in the Water," although logically incorrect, was, on another level, an allegory "That doth instruct the Mind/ In things that ly behind," a hieroglyph symbolizing a deeper reality (ll. 1-6).[6] In the same way, Traherne accepted the orthodox doctrine of the Fall on one level while acknowledging on another level the psychological approximation of the State of Innocence in the mind of the child.

Although all humanity is necessarily involved in original sin, Traherne recalled how as a child he was insulated by his very ignorance and temporarily spared any knowledge of the pain and corruption around him.   In "Eden," he pointed out how this "learned and . . . Happy Ignorance/ Divided me" from all of the "madness and the Miserie/ Of Men" (ll. 1-2, 5-6). He explained in the Centuries that this "very Ignorance was advantageous," for, unaware of the existence of sin, sickness, division, and discord, he neither perceived them nor experienced them.

A child, Traherne maintained, sees "all Things . . . Spotless and Pure and Glorious" simply because he knows nothing else. Unaware of division in time or in space, he sees "Boys and Girles Tumbling in the Street" as "moving Jewels" and knows "not that they were Born or should Die." Sheltered by his innocence from a knowledge of corruption and mutability, he sees "Every thing. . . at Rest, Free and Immortal." He knows "nothing of Sickness or Death or Exaction." Like Adam before the Fall, the child knows no threat of change, no danger of loss. Free from the desperation a sense of time brings to his postlapsarian parents, the child contentedly sees "all in the Peace of Eden" (C III:2).

Traherne's descriptions of the child's edenic world view and unconscious oneness with all things are not only unique for his time, but they also anticipate recent observations on the psychology of childhood. One's sense of identity, according to C.G. Jung, "derives essentially from the notorious unconsciousness" of childhood, a state of "non-differentiation," in which "there is as yet no clearly differentiated ego."[7] The child-speaker in many of Traherne's poems seems to be in such an oceanic state, unconscious of its own physical limitations. Such is the impression conveyed by "The Preparative":

> My Body being Dead, my Lims unknown;
> > Before I skild to prize
> > Those living Stars mine Eys,
> Before my Tongue or Cheeks were to me shewn,
> > Before I knew my Hands were mine,
> Or that my Sinews did my Members joyn,
> > When neither Nostril, Foot, nor Ear
> As yet was seen, or felt, or did appear;
> > I was within
> A House I knew not, newly clothd with Skin.
>
> Then was my Soul my only All to be
> > A Living Endless Ey
> > Far wider then the Skie.

(ll. 1-13)

According to psychologists, the child is at first "not even aware of its own body limits." His hands and feet he sees as objects, not as part of himself.[8] This again concurs with the initial stage of perception described by Traherne as the State of Innocence. Before time and limits are known to the child, he is unaware of where his individual self stops and the rest

80

of the world begins. Then, ("My Body being Dead, my Lims unknown; . . . Before I knew my Hands were mine") the child is conscious only of an expansive sense of harmony and well-being.

As Traherne explained in the Centuries, the child in his innocence perceives a unity and goodness in all things:

> All appeared New, and Strange at the first, inexpressibly
> rare and Delightfull, and Beautifull. I was a little Stranger,
> which at my Enterance into the World was Saluted and
> Surrounded with Innumerable Joys. My Knowledg was
> Divine. I knew by Intuition those things which since my
> Apostasie I Collected again by the Highest Reason. . . .
> All things were Spotles and Pure and Glorious: yea, and
> infinitly mine, and Joyfull and Precious. I knew not that
> there were any Sins, or Complaints or Laws. (C III:2)

Everything appears new and wondrous to the child, who is fascinated by the ordinary and everyday objects adults take for granted.[9] Instead of compartmentalizing experience in terms of function as adults do almost automatically, the child, with no labels to attach to things, sees them in esthetic terms as color, texture, and form. This kind of perception is possible for adults when the process of automatic classification is thwarted by a rearrangement of experience, as in art, or in life, in states of altered or expanded consciousness, when objects are displaced, magnified to the extreme, or somehow divested of normal sequence. Such is the perception of wonder Traherne sought to convey in his works. Casting the light of glory upon the everyday with his art, he hoped to undo in part the process of classification and limitation fostered by civilization, and reawaken in his readers the pure vision of childhood when:

> The Corn was Orient and Immortal Wheat, which never
> should be reaped, nor was ever sown. I thought it had
> stood from everlasting to everlasting. The Dust and
> Stones of the Street were as Precious as GOLD. The
> Gates were at first the End of the World. The Green
> Trees when I saw them first through one of the Gates
> Transported and Ravished me; their Sweetnes and unusual
> Beauty made my Heart to leap, and almost mad with Ex-
> tasie, they were such strange and Wonderfull Things: The
> Men! O What Venerable and Reverend Creaturs did the
> Aged seem! Immortal Cherubins! And yong Men Glittering
> and Sparkling Angels and Maids strange Seraphick Pieces
> of Life and Beauty! Boys and Girls Tumbling in the Street,
> and Playing, were moving Jewels. I knew not that they
> were Born or should Die. But all things abided Eternally
> as they were in their Proper Places. Eternity was Mani-
> fest in the Light of the Day, and som thing infinit Behind
> evry thing appeared: which talked with my Expectation
> and moved my Desire. The Citie seemd to stand in Eden,
> or to be Built in Heaven.   (C III:3).

As Traherne affirmed repeatedly, the child "nothing in the World did know,/ But 'twas Divine." His own body as well as the world around him he perceives in terms of harmony, experiencing "A Native Health and Innocence/ Within [his] Bones" ("Wonder," ll. 23-24, 17-18). Unaware of pain and sickness, ugliness and inadequacy, the child knows no physical shame. On the contrary, he rejoices in his body as a gift from God, seeing

> New Burnisht Joys!
> Which yellow Gold and Pearl excell!
> Such Sacred Treasures are the Lims in Boys,
> In which a Soul doth Dwell;
> Their Organized Joynts, and Azure Veins
> More Wealth include, then all the World contains.

("The Salutation," ll. 19-24)

As one presumably knows no tension or embarrassment prior to ego-development,[10] so Traherne also noted the absence of these problems in early childhood when, unable to distinguish between his body and soul, the individual experiences "A Vigour in [his] Sence/ That was all SPIRIT" ("Wonder," ll. 20-21). Temporarily blessed with a unified sensibility, the child, he realized, bears none of the agonizing conflicts of body and soul that beset fallen adults.

As we have seen, Traherne described the child as fascinated by himself and his body. Ignorant of the "serious business of life," the child-speaker in his works fails to measure the things he sees around him by utilitarian or economic standards: he merely perceives them as objects of delight. In addition, Traherne portrayed his own childhood as a time free from unfulfilled needs.[11] In "The Preparative," for example, he recalled that "No dull Necessity,/ No Want was known to me;" (ll. 22-23). With all of his needs anticipated by the benevolent family around him, the child, Traherne concluded, knows "no Thirst nor Hunger," no conflict between desire and reality on even the most basic of levels (l. 21).

Traherne realized that childhood is a time when everything seems spread before our eyes in a panorama for our enjoyment. With no conflicts between desire and reality, the child knows no want; ignorant of the notion of private property, he feels no poverty. Instead, the child's expansive self claims all that he perceives. Traherne recalled how in childhood he had felt

> as High and Great,
> As Kings are in their Seat.
> All other Things were mine.
> The World my House, the Creatures were my Goods,
> Fields, Mountains, Valleys, Woods,
> Floods, Cities, Churches, Men, for me did shine.

("Speed," ll. 13-18)

This limitless sense of self pervades Traherne's works. In the Centuries, for example, he sought to recreate the ecstatic vision of childhood when "The Streets were mine, the Temple was mine, the People were mine, their Clothes and Gold and Silver were mine, as much as their Sparkling Eys Fair Skins and ruddy faces. The Skies were mine, and so the Sun and Moon and Stars, and all the World was mine, and I the only Spectator and Enjoyer of it. I knew no Churlish Proprieties, nor Bounds nor Division: but all Proprieties and Divisions were mine: all Treasures and the Possessors of them" (C III:3).

Again, until the child becomes consciously separate from his mother and the world she represents, modern studies have shown that he feels an expansive oneness with all things.[12] This sensation Traherne also recognized as peculiar to childhood. For example, in "My Spirit" he recalled:

> I felt no Dross nor Matter in my Soul,
> Nor Brims nor Borders, such as in a Bowl
> We see, My Essence was Capacitie.
>   That felt all Things.

(ll. 6-9)

In a later passage he states: "My Soul . . . / was Indivisible and so Pure,/ That all my Mind was wholy Evry where" (ll. 54-56).

For Traherne this apprehension of infinite oneness was a matter of human instinct. "We first by Nature all things boundless see;/ Feel all illimited," he stated; but once exposed to the values of civilization, "we are taught/ To limit and to bound our Thought" ("The City," ll. 61-62, 69-70). Again, in the Centuries, Traherne maintained, "Few will believ the Soul to be infinit: yet Infinit is the first Thing which is naturally Known. Bounds and Limits are Discerned only in a Secondary manner" (C II: 81). Centuries before Jung and others announced such theories, Traherne observed that the child's first sensation was an expansive, unconscious union with all creation. He realized that this perception was intuitive and faded with the dawn of reason and language in the individual. In his poem "Dumnesse" he recalled a time when

> nothing spoke to me but the fair Face
> Of Heav'n and Earth, before my self could speak,
> I then my Bliss did, when my Silence, break.

(ll. 18-20)

And his observations are confirmed by Jung's statement that "Scarcely has speech developed when, in next to no time, consciousness is present; and this with its momentary contents and its memories, exercises an intensive check upon the previous collective contents."[13]

This initial perception of harmony in childhood, although later effaced by the development of consciousness, remains with all individuals in the depths of their memory. This Traherne realized long before the advent of modern psychology, as he portrayed in his works a pattern basic to human existence. Each of us experiences in childhood a brief period of "innocence," sheltered by our youth from the demands of reality, protected and nourished by the all-encompassing love of our parents. This experience remains with us throughout life, impossible to recapture, yet equally impossible to forget. Committed to this world, yet desiring to return to another, we are left with an eternal nostalgia for the lost paradise of our youth. Realizing that the concept of the four estates represented actual stages of consciousness, Traherne emphasized the parallel between the historical and individual States of Innocence throughout his works. By reminding his readers of the joyous sensations they had experienced in childhood, he hoped to awaken in them a longing for the lost joys of Eden which cannot be satisfied in this fallen world, and lead them to seek fulfillment in their conversion to the State of Grace.

Misery

As we have seen, Traherne believed that the fall into the State of Misery was a phase of individual development beginning with the age of reason in the child. As he had declared in the Centuries, "The first Light which shined in my Infancy in its Primitive and Innocent Clarity was totaly ecclypsed; insomuch that I was fain to learn all again" (C III:7). Recently, psychologists have also described such a state of alienation and division as part of "the normal evolution of character," arising with the development of ego-awareness in early adolescence."[14] Traherne, however, felt that the child is misled by the corrupt customs and manners around him, which pervert his original set of values, distorting his perception of himself and the world. "It was a Difficult matter to persuade me that the Tinsild Ware upon a Hobby hors was a fine thing," he recalled. But "They did impose upon me, and Obtrude their gifts that made me believ a Ribban or a Feather Curious. I could not see where was the Curiousness or fineness: And to Teach me that A Purs of Gold was of any valu seemed impossible, the Art by which it becomes so, and the reasons for which it is accounted so were so Deep and Hidden to my Inexperience" (C III:9). Yet, he explained, the child's perception is soon corrupted "by the Customs and maners of Men" (C III:7). This point he portrayed more fully in his poem "Poverty," which recalls how he was blinded to the truth of his identity as a child of God:

As in the House I sate
Alone and desolate
No Creature but the Fire and I,
The Chimney and the Stool, I lift mine Ey
Up to the Wall,
And in the Silent Hall
Saw nothing mine
But som few Cups and Dishes shine
The Table and the wooden Stools
Where Peeple us'd to dine:

A painted Cloth there was
Wherin som ancient Story wrought
A little entertain'd my Thought
Which Light discover'd throu the Glass.

I wonder'd much to see
That all my Wealth should be
Confin'd in such a little Room,
Yet hope for more I scarcely durst presume
It griev'd me sore
That such a scanty Store
Should be my All:
For I forgat my Eas and Health,
Nor did I think of Hands or Eys.
Nor Soul nor Body prize;
I neither thought the Sun,
Nor Moon, nor Stars, nor Peeple, mine,
Tho they did round about me shine;
And therfore was I quite undon.

(ll. 1-28)

His loneliness and desolation heightened by the poverty he sees around him, the child speaker in this poem is "Confin'd in such a little Room," not by actuality but by his narrowness of thought. He is unaware of the treasures of his body and soul, the moon, sun, and stars, and the whole world shining about him. Limited by a narrow and artificial definition of wealth, the child, as Traherne has pointed out, is not so much materially as spiritually poor.

Traherne saw misery as alienation, not only from the world, but from God and one's identity in the divine plan. "To be alone in the World was to be Desolate and Miserable" (C III:23) Traherne declared in the Centuries and in his poem "Solitude" he again depicted this kind of alienation:

How desolate!
Ah! how forlorn, how sadly did I stand
When in the field my woful State
I felt! Not all the Land,
Not all the Skies,
Tho Heven shin'd before mine Eys,
Could Comfort yield in any Field to me,
Nor could my Mind Contentment find or see.

(ll. 1-8)

In his poem, "Misapprehension," Traherne complained that too many people live in such spiritual poverty:

Men are not wise in their Tru Interest,
Nor in the Worth of what they long possest:
   They know no more what is their Own
   Than they the Valu of't have known.
      They pine in Misery,
      Complain of Poverty,
      Reap not where they hav sown,
      Griev for Felicity,
      Blaspheme the Deity;
  And all becaus they are not blest
  With Eys to see the Worth of Things:
For did they know their Reall Interest,
   No doubt they'd all be Kings.

(ll. 1-13)

For Traherne, sin and Misery were a falling away from our original sense of oneness with the universe into blindness and spiritual oblivion: "Sin is a Moral Obliquity, and the change it produceth in the Soul is Spiritual. It makes a Man to differ far more from himself, than any alteration of Body can do; but withal so blinds his Understanding, that he does not remember what he was in his first Parents" (CE, p. 37). Traherne abjured material treasures because they "put Grubs and Worms in Mens Heads: that are Enemies to all Pure and True Apprehensions, and eat out all their Happines. . . . They alienat men from the Life of GOD, and at last make them to live without GOD in the World" (C III:13).

Right apprehension was a matter of vital importance to Traherne, for sin and misery he believed were largely the result of misapprehension. He explained in Christian Ethicks that as we perceive the world, so we receive from it, recognizing that "a discontented mind [can] disorder the Soul, or disturb the World." It makes of an individual his own worst enemy, "an unwelcome Creature to himself till he can [again] delight in his condition and know himself as a child of God" (p. 216).

"The World," he realized, "is both a Paradice and a Prison to different Persons," depending on their frames of mind (C I:76). Thus, he attempted to lead his readers from Misery to the State of Grace by repairing their fallen apprehension, constantly exhorting them to "Enjoy the World aright," to see it in spiritual terms, as a gift of God, and not to be limited by the meager terms of private property. All the streets, the people of the city and all of the world--the ocean, sun and stars--were theirs to enjoy, as Traherne proclaimed: "You never Enjoy the World, till the Sea it self floweth in your Veins, till you are Clothed with the Heavens, and Crowned with the Stars: and Perceiv yourself to be the Sole Heir of the whole world" (C I:29).

Grace

The State of Grace for Traherne was a process of spiritual alchemy in which, by God's grace and their own efforts, people's eyes were opened and the dross purged away to reveal the divine truth behind all existence. However, for Traherne, the State of Grace was also a "State of Trial" in which one must work to reform his fallen perceptions, searching for truth amid darkness and confusion. For one must "learn a Diviner Art that wil now be Happy: and that is like a Royal Chymist to reign among Poysons to turn Scorpions into fishes, Weeds into flowers, Bruises into Ornaments, Poysons into Cordials. . . . now a Man must like a GOD, bring Light out of Darkness, and Order out of Confusion. Which we are taught to do by His Wisdom, that Ruleth in the midst of Storms and Tempests" (C IV:21). Yet Traherne saw this Trial in a positive light. "This Estate wherein I am placed is the Best for me: tho Encompassed with Difficulties" (C IV: 89), he believed, for Trial was an exercise of one's virtue and one's free will.

Unlike the Calvinists, who saw the individual as a helpless pawn in God's game of sin and salvation, Traherne emphasized our free will and self-determination. God granted us the grace of Redemption, but gave us the dignity of choice, the responsibility for our own fate, he explained: "God gave us Liberty, in the beginning, that we might chuse what we would, and placed us in such an Estate; that, having in us only the Seeds and Principles of all Vertue, we might exercise our natural Power of our own Accord, for the Attainment of that actual Knowledge, Wisdom and Righteousness, wherein the Perfection of our soul consisteth" (CE, p. 231). Traherne felt that the attainment of grace was an "art," requiring an active effort on the part of the individual. As he wrote in the Meditations on the Six Days of the Creation, "It is not enough, that we have our Calling from God, but we must make it sure with good Works too."[15]

In agreement with most seventeenth-century theologians, Traherne believed that calling was the first stage in conversion, but felt that unless one actively answered God's call with prayer and meditation he would not be saved. He saw Grace as a process uniting the human will with the divine: God "Willed the Redemption of Mankind, and therfore is His Son Jesus Christ an infinit Treasure." But, he believed, Grace must also be a personal experience: "Unless you will it too, He will be no Treasure to you" (C I:53), for God "desireth that [each man] should by Prayers and Endeavors clothe [him]self with Grace" (C IV:88).

Prevenient grace, Traherne saw as a measure of renewed vision brought by the Holy Ghost, "Illuminating, Strengthening and Comforting the Soul of the Seer" (C II:45). His poem "Com Holy Ghost Eternal God" asks God for this grace:

Com Holy Ghost Eternal God
   Our Hearts with Life Inspire
Inkindle Zeal in all our Souls
And fill us with thy Heavenly fire.

Send forth thy Beams, and Let thy Grace
   Upon my Spirit shine:
That I may all thy Works enjoy,
Revive, Sing Praises, be Divine.

(ll. 1-8)

As the poem shows, Traherne also believed that after enlightenment by
the Holy Ghost, people must participate in their regeneration. They must
"Sing Praises," pray and meditate, actively pursuing their own salvation.

   Penance played a part in Traherne's view of Grace and conversion,
but it was not the focal point of his works, for he emphasized instead the
love of God and the gifts or "Treasures" he showers on us. Still, Traherne
acknowledged penance as the next step in the process of obtaining grace,
after our "calling" from God. As he declared in Christian Ethicks, "Repentance is the Beginning of that Life wherein all the sweat and Labour
of the Martyrs, all the Persecutions and Endeavours of the Apostles, all
the Revelations of the Prophets, all the examples of the Patriarchs, all
the Miracles of old Time, all the Mysteries of the Law, all the Means of
Grace, all the Verities of the Gospel begin to take full force and Effect,
in obtaining that for which they were intended" (pp. 128-29). Some of
Traherne's works record prayers to and colloquies with God, in which the
speaker displays the conviction, contrition, and confession found in Donne
or Herbert. For example, in Meditations on the Six Days of the Creation,
Traherne declared:

For Shame then, O my guilty Soul, begin
To weep, lament, and wash away thy Sin.
   Begin before it be too late;
   Beg pardon for thy Faults so great;
Repent, amend thy Life, amend thy Ways.
He's blest that his Creator's Will obeys.

And since to please thee nothing I can do
Without thy Grace, thy Grace do thou bestow.
   O God, that furnish'd I may be
   With sufficient Strength from thee,
To conquer all Temptations that arise
To whatever sort of Sin, or Vice.

(p. 91; ll. 55-72, italics rev.)

   Yet within the body of Traherne's works such penetential passages
are rare, for Traherne believed that the way to Grace was not paved primarily with pain and suffering, but with joy and a gradual spiritual unfold-
ment. In his works the latter clearly predominates; as he declared at the
beginning of the Centuries, he did not intend to frighten people into religion by tales of hell and damnation, but, rather, to reveal to them the
signs of God's love: "I will not by the Nois of Bloody Wars, and the De-
throning of Kings, advance you to Glory: but by the Gentle Ways of Peace

and Love. As a Deep Friendship meditats and intends the Deepest De-
signes for the Advancement of its Objects . . . so God, Designing to shew
his Lov in exalting you hath chosen the Ways of Eas and Repose, by which
you should ascend" (C I:4). Influenced, as Louis Martz has shown, by Sa-
lesian meditation, which promotes serenity and peace of mind,[16] Traherne's works show none of the anguish and passionate struggle of Ignatian
meditation, well exemplified by Donne. Traherne's purpose was instead
"to elevate the Soul . . . and guide Men (that stand in need of help) in the
way of Vertue; to excite their Desire, to encourage them to Travel, to
comfort them in the Journey, and so at last to lead them to true Felicity,
both here and hereafter." He intended to portray virtue and the pathway
to Grace as so attractive that no one could refuse, maintaining, "my business is to make as visible, as it is possible for me, the lustre of [the]
Beauty, Dignity, and Glory [of Felicity]. By shewing what a necessary
means Vertue is, how sweet, how full of Reason, how desirable in it self,
how just and amiable, how delightful, and how powerfully conducive . . .
to Glory" (CE. p. 3).

Leading people into Grace was, for Traherne, primarily a matter of
educating them in right apprehension. "Tis not Change of Place but Glorious Principles well Practised that establish Heaven in the Life and Soul,"
he said in the Centuries (IV:37). Grace for him involved a vision of the
world illuminated by "Glorious Principles"; Misery, on the other hand, was
darkness and ignorance. Traherne realized that "a little Grit in the Ey
destroyeth the sight of the very Heavens, and a little Malice or Envy a
World of Joys" (C IV:17), and labored to bring his readers the harmonious
apprehension of the State of Grace, certain that "Were there no Blindness,
every Soul would be full of Light, and the face of Felicity be seen, and
the Earth be turned into Heaven" (CE, p. 4).

Like Richard Baxter, who held that "close meditation on the matter
and cause of our Joy, is Gods way to procure solid Joy,"[17] Traherne believed in the importance of meditation, which he saw as a creative process with which fallen men and women might piece together their fragmented apprehension of the world and achieve a renewal of spiritual harmony. Since Traherne felt that the source of our misery was largely subjective, he believed that by meditating and putting their soul in order,
people might effect a change in their entire estate, "If any thing were
amiss," Traherne stated in the Centuries, a man should consult "his own
heart, and [will find] nothing but that out of frame.by restoring which al
things were rectified, and made Delightfull. As much as that had swerved
from the Rule of Justice Equity and Right, so far was he miserable" (C
IV:41).

Well-versed in the meditative tradition, Traherne felt that one could
come to a higher spiritual consciousness by meditating on the two books
left to him by God: the book of God's Word (the Bible) and the Book of
God's Works (Nature). In the Centuries (III:29) Traherne related how he
discovered his spiritual identity by reading and meditating on the Bible.
His poem "The Bible" also reflects the joy of his discovery:

89

there I was told
That I the Son of God was made,
His Image. O Divine! And that fine Gold,
With all the Joys that here do fade,
Are but a Toy, compared to the Bliss
Which Hev'nly, God-like, and Eternal is.
That We on earth are Kings;
And, tho' we're cloath'd with mortal Skin,
And Inward Cherubins; hav Angels Wings;
Affections, Thoughts, and Minds within.

(ll. 1-10)

Reading the Bible, he relates, purified his vision, revealing to him the treasures created for mankind in the State of Innocence, treasures that remain ours in this world if only we recognize them:

> there I was Adam in Paradice, surrounded with the Beauty of Heaven and Earth, void of all Earthly Comforts, to wit such as were devised, Gorgeous Apparel, Palaces, Gold and Silver, Coaches, Musical Instruments, &c., And entertained only with Celestial Joys. The sun and moon and stars, Beasts and fowles and fishes, Trees and fruits, and flowers, with the other Naked and simple Delights of Nature. By which I evidently saw that the Way to becom Rich and Blessed was not by heaping Accidental and Devised Riches to make ourselvs great in the vulgar maner, but to approach more near and to see more Clearly with the Ey of our understanding, the Beauties and Glories of the whole world: and to hav communion with the Deity in the Riches of GOD and Nature.
>
> (C III:67)

Meditating on the Bible, Traherne maintained, repairs our fallen apprehension and enables us to see beyond brittle material values to the treasures created by God: "For when all the Things are gone which Men can giv, A Man is still as Rich as Adam was in Eden: who was Naked there. A Naked man is the Richest Creature in all Worlds: and can never be Happy; till he sees the Riches of his Nakedness. He is very Poor in Knowledg that thinks Adam poor in Eden" (C IV:36), Traherne concluded.

But while he meditated on both the Bible and creation, in his works, the overwhelming number of Bonaventuran meditations on nature clearly illustrates his own predilection, revealing his great love for the natural world. Unlike many Christians, Traherne's religious ferver did not involve an ascetic renunciation of the world, a contemptus mundi, but a fuller enjoyment of the natural world as a manifestation of God's infinite love for humanity. Conscious of his departure from tradition in urging men to "Enjoy the World," he explained his position in the Centuries, questioning the religious conviction of those who contemn the world and "place and desire all their Happiness in another life." He wondered "Whether the first sort be Christians indeed," maintaining that since God has offered us happiness in this life, "they that put of[f] felicity with long delays, are to be much suspected. for it is against the Nature of Lov and desire to defer" (C IV:9).

In another passage, Traherne clarified what he meant by exhorting people to "Enjoy the World." "Truly there are two Worlds," he explained. "One was made by God, the other by Men. That made by GOD, was Great and Beautifull. Before the Fall, it was Adams Joy, and the Temple of his Glory. That made by men is a Babel of Confusions: Invented Riches, Pomps, and Vanities, brought in by Sin. . . . Leav the one that you may enjoy the other" (C I:7), he counseled his readers, encouraging them to forsake the tinseled creations of men, the artificial riches of Misery, for the infinite treasures of God.

The natural world, for Traherne, remained largely unfallen, its apparent corruption resting more in human apprehension than in reality. When seen correctly, he maintained, it "is the Paradice of God. It is more to Man since he is faln, then it was before. It is the Place of Angels, and the Gate of Heaven" (C I:31). Yet to be so enjoyed, the world must be perceived spiritually as well as physically; we must read the Divine Hieroglyphs written for us in the Book of Nature. "You are never your true self, till you live by your Soul more then by your Body" (C II:92), maintained Traherne, exhorting his readers to grasp the spiritual significance of all they experienced. "Pigs eat Acorns," he explained, "but neither consider the Sun that gav them Life, not the Influences of the Heavens by which they were Nourished, nor the very Root of the Tree from whence they came. This being the Work of Angels, Who . . . feed upon that Acorn Spiritually while they Know the Ends for which it was Created and feast upon all these, as upon a World of Joys within it" (C I:26). Anything less, Traherne contended, limits a human being to his animal nature. To love God is to meditate upon the world, to know it spiritually, to "feed with Pleasure upon evry Thing that is His. So that the World shall be a Grand Jewel of Delight unto you: a very Paradice, and the Gate of Heaven" (C I:20).

As we have seen, Traherne believed that the child is born with apprehensions of wonder and delight. Unaware of economic values, and corruption, he perceives the world intuitively, experiencing a harmony similar to that known by Adam in paradise. Traherne attributed this early apprehension of infinity to Divine Providence, believing that God placed the individual in a personal State of Innocence as part of his plan of salvation. Paralleling the first estate of every individual with the first estate of Christian mankind, God implants all men and women with an instinctive awareness of their spiritual identity. And when through custom and error they fall away from this sense of unity, they are left with an inherent longing for a return to the primal harmony they have experienced. As Traherne declared in "Innocence,"

91

The anchient Light of Eden did convey
Into my Soul: I was an Adam there,
    A little Adam in a Sphere
    Of Joys! O there my Ravisht Sence
Was entertained in Paradice,
And had a Sight of Innocence
All was beyond all Bound and Price.

An Antepast of Heaven sure!
    I on the Earth did reign.
Within, without me, all was pure.
I must becom a Child again.

(ll. 50-60)

This yearning for a retreat to a lost innocence is also found in the poetry of Henry Vaughan. In "The Retreate" he looked back to "those early dayes! when I/ Shin'd in my Angell-infancy":

O how I long to travell back
And tread again that ancient track!
That I might once more reach that plaine,
Where first I left my glorious traine,
From whence th'Inlightned spirit sees
That shady City of Palm trees;
But (ah!) my soul with too much stay
Is drunk, and staggers in the way,
Some men a forward motion love,
But I by backward steps would move,
And when this dust falls to the urn
In that state I came return.

(ll. 1-2, 21-32)

However, although both men described the innocence of childhood and their desire to regain it, their works reveal a significant difference in tone. Vaughan's verses are, for the most part, limited to brief descriptions of innocence punctuated with colloquies in which the speaker cries out in near-desperation, asking God to come and forcibly take him away from this miserable world and return him to a state of primal bliss. Traherne was less Calvinistic than Vaughan. Believing as he did in the individual's ability to approach grace actively by exercising his soul in meditation, Traherne has none of Vaughan's desperate urgency. More objective, more analytical, he concentrated on describing for his readers his own states of consciousness. To some extent influenced by the attitude of the Royal Society, Traherne held that people could use their minds and put them in frame much better when they knew more about them. Thus, Traherne's descriptions of his own mental processes can be seen as an attempt to give his readers practical information on the workings of the greatest tool God had given them, in order that they might best use their minds in meditation and fulfill themselves as spiritual beings.

In this poem in the Centuries, he explained to his readers that the thoughts implanted in each individual in childhood are part of God's plan, revealing to each individual what their state was in paradise and what they could achieve on a higher level with God's grace:

These Thoughts His Goodness long before
Prepar'd as Precious and Celestial Store:
   With Curious Art in me inlaid,
That Childhood might it self alone be said
   My Tutor Teacher Guid to be,
Instructed then even by the Deitie.

(III:4)

Looking back again to his own childhood, Traherne counseled his readers on how they too might regain the sense of harmony they had once known intuitively by perceiving the world "aright" through the gift of reason. God, Traherne emphasized, was present in all creation: "He is Himself in evry Thing.som Things are little on the outside, and Rough and Common. but I remember the Time, when the Dust of the Streets were as precious as Gold to my Infant Eys, and now they are more precious to the Ey of Reason" (C I:25). To "Enjoy the World aright" is to perceive divinity everywhere, to commune with God in an expansive oneness similar to that felt by a small child, except that the adult vision of harmony is a conscious state, seen "through the Ey of Reason." As he explained in the Centuries, "the World is a Pomgranat indeed, which GOD hath put into mans Heart, as Solomon observeth in the Ecclesiastes, becaus it containeth the Seeds of Grace and the Seeds of Glory. All Virtues lie in the World, as Seeds in a Pomegranate" (C II:96). Our duty, then, is to discover these virtues, meditate on them, and expand our souls in the grace of integrated consciousness as we perceive the divine pattern in all existence.

Ultimately, then, Traherne felt that by meditating upon the Bible and nature, an individual might regain in the State of Grace the oneness with creation he had experienced in the State of Innocence on an even higher level of joy and awareness. By enjoying God's works, he explained, "Thou Expandest and Enlargest thy self" (C I:73). Thus, the individual would achieve Regeneration, which Traherne saw as an expansive communion with God and all creation, when "all Ages are present in my Soul, and all Kingdoms, and GOD Blessed forever. And thus Jesus Christ is seen in me and dwelleth in me, when I believ upon Him.And thus all Saints are in me, and I in them. And thus all Angels and the Eternity and Infinity of GOD are in me for evermore. I being the Living TEMPLE and Comprehensor of them" (C I:100). In a prayer of thanksgiving, he praised Jesus for redeeming him to this state and for restoring him "to the Friendship of GOD, to the Enjoyment of the World, To the Hope of Eternal Glory, To the Lov of Angels Cherubims and Men . . . . abov all to the Image of GOD" (C I:76).

Traherne believed that only in the State of Grace, when he is restored to the image of God, can the individual fully accomplish his

93

purpose within the divine plan. We were given intelligence and free will so that we might mirror God's gifts in apprehension and thanksgiving, reflecting the love manifested in creation back again to the Creator. As he explained, "the Idea of Heaven and Earth in the Soul of Man, is more Precious with GOD than the Things them selves and more Excellent in nature. . . . what would Heaven and Earth be worth, were there no Spectator, no Enjoyer? As much therfore as the End is better than the Means, the Thought of the World wherby it is Enjoyed is Better than the World. So is the Idea of it in the Soul of Man, better then the World in the Esteem of GOD: It being the End of the World, without which Heaven and Earth would be in vain" (C II:90). Thus, Traherne encouraged his readers to meditate, to refine their apprehension, and to seek the State of Grace: "lov God Angels and Men, Triumph in Gods Works, delight in Gods Laws, Take Pleasure in Gods Ways in all Ages, Correct Sins, bring good out of evill, subdue your Lusts, order your sences, Conquer the Customs and Opinions of men, and render Good for evil," he told his readers, and "you are in Heaven evry where" (C IV:38).

Glory

The State of Glory represented for Traherne the culmination of the Felicity begun in the State of Grace. He saw this state as both individual and historical, incorporating "the Nature of Seperat Souls" after death, and the historical "Resurrection of the Body, the Day of Judgment, and Life Everlasting. Wherin further we are to see and understand the Communion of Saints, Heavenly Joys, and our Society with Angels" (C III:43).

Like other theologians of his time, Traherne wrote about God's "Judgment of the World, [his] Punishment of his Enemies, [and] the Rewarding of his friends, in Eternal Glory" (C III:100). However, even as he acknowledged God's "Punishment of his Enemies," he emphasized God's mercy in all of his works. His descriptions of the Last Judgment refer, by necessity, to punitive justice, but quickly move on, to dwell with ecstatic delight on God's "Rewarding of his friends, in Eternal Glory." For, as we have seen, Traherne stressed the positive aspects of religion, attempting to draw people toward Heaven by "the Gentle Ways of Peace and Lov" rather than by frightening them with the fiery torments of hell (C I:4).

Reflecting this attitude, his works abound with references to the promise of consummate bliss in the final State of Glory, where "Love, and Joy, and Gratitude will be all that will continue for ever, in which Estate, Wisdom and Knowledge, Goodness and Righteousness, and true Holiness shall abide, as the Life and Glory into which the souls of all that are Blessed will be transformed" (CE, p. 35). Like Anselmus, Traherne believed that at the Resurrection the bodies of the faithful will be glorified in all aspects. "Health, Agility, Beauty, Vivacity, Strength, and Liberty," Traherne declared, shall then be enjoyed (CE, p. 18).

"Glory is the perfection of Beauty," he asserted, and this, of course, meant spiritual beauty as well. In Glory "Righteousness and Holiness, and Goodness and Charity shall with all the rest be the Lineaments and Colours of the Mind, the Graces and Beauties of the blessed Soul: They shall shine upon its face, and it self shall be glorious in the perfection of their Beauty, as GOD is" (CE, p. 86). Glorified in body and soul, the individual in this final estate will shine in goodness like the sun and stars, his vision illuminating all that stands before him. In Traherne's words, "Like the Sun we [will] dart our Rayes before us, and occupy those Spaces with Light and Contemplation, which we move towards, but possess not with our Bodies. And seeing all Things in the Light of Divine Knowledg, eternally serving God, rejoyce unspeakably in that service, and enjoy it all" (C V:8). Traherne, like other theological writers, stressed the divine wisdom that will be ours in the State of Glory when God's Wisdome shall be our Wisdom" (CE, p. 70), and human knowledge will expand to encompass "all that the light of Heaven and Eternity can reveal" (CE, p. 177).

Traherne saw the communion of saints as one of the most joyous aspects of the State of Glory, when the individual soul will expand to enjoy not merely his own glorification, but the reflection of those around him. There, finally, people will be able to rejoyce in their own good fortune without pride and others will admire them without envy. As he explained in the Centuries, "We shall there enjoy the Happiness of being seen in Happinesse, without the Danger of Ostentation" (C IV:12). There "evry Soul being full, and fully satisfied, at Eas, in rest, and Wanting nothing, easily overflows and shines upon all. . . . Self Love there being swallowed up and made perfect in the Lov of others" (C IV:60). In the State of Glory, men and women shall delight, without selfishness, in the beauty they find in themselves and in one another, "All there being like so many Suns Shining upon one" (C IV:85). In Heaven the individual's happiness will be amplified, not diminished, by the knowledge that everyone else is exalted in the same manner as himself. Shining upon each other with love, the glorified will reflect like so many mirrors, the image and the love of God. For Traherne, Heaven was more than a region of light; it was ablaze with reflections, a galaxy of souls, each one as beautiful as the next.

The joys of Heaven will be infinite and eternal. There we shall "hav the Joy of seeing our selvs Eternaly beloved, and Eternaly Blessed, and infinitely Enjoying all the Parts of our Blessedness" (C V:8). The pleasures in the State of Glory will be totally different from those of this world, for then man will be blessed with "outward Security, and inward Contentment" (CE, p. 197), whereas now people are restless, driven by appetites which nothing in this world seems to satisfy. On earth, Traherne explained, "men get one Hundred Pound a year that they may get another; and having two covet Eight; and there is no End of all their Labor; because the Desire of their Soul is Insatiable" (C I:22). People are restless, he believed, because their appetites are celestially oriented and they are "for ever to be displeased unless [their] glory and blessedness be Eternal" (CE, p. 220). But in Glory our desires will be satisfied and we will find ourselves at peace. Completely fulfilled by the joys of paradise, our restlessness will cease at last. Furthermore, Traherne maintained, souls in Glory will no longer by subject to temptation, "For in the King-dom of Glory it is impossible to fall. No man can sin that clearly seeth the beauty of Gods face: Becaus no Man can sin against his own Happi-ness" (C II:97).

Glory for Traherne signified above all the culmination of the indivi-dual's friendship with God, a never-ending exchange of divine love for hu-man. All the delights of Heaven, he maintained, "would be of little avail" were it not for this complete communion of souls and hearts, which re-fines and glorifies the soul of man: "By Love the Soul is transformed into the Similtude of God, by Love made Bright and Beautiful, and its Blessed-ness and Glory are founded in its Love" (CE, p. 56). "It is not the Love of God to us, so much as our love to his, that maketh Heaven," he ex-plained, for the love of God, already perfect, needs only the perfected love of human souls to make the circle complete (CE, p. 31).

By manifesting divine love, one fulfills his potential as a son and heir of God and is able "To sit in the Throne of GOD and to enjoy Com-munion with him" (CE, p. 55). By this love, the individual is brought closer to God, where he sees "no more in a Glass, but Face to Face," and knows as he is known (CE, p. 142), transformed into the perfect image of his Creator. Throughout his works, Traherne looked ahead to this point beyond time, when he, like all the redeemed, was "to be Partaker of the Divine Nature, to be filled with all the Fulness of GOD, to enter into his Kingdom and Glory, to be transformed into his Image, and made an Heir of GOD, and a joynt Heir with Christ, to live in Union and Communion with GOD." This, he realized, was the final state of human souls, "the Perfection of their Bliss and Happiness" (CE, p. 22), and he held out this vision to his readers as the ultimate promise in their evolution of con-sciousness as they followed him in their journey through the four estates.

NOTES

[1]Centuries, Poems and Thanksgivings, ed. H.M. Margoliouth (Oxford: Clarendon Press, 1958), I. All references to the Centuries (C) are from this edition and will hereafter be abbreviated in the text.

[2]Centuries, Poems and Thanksgivings, II, 37-39. (ll. 7-8, 23-24, 25-26). All of Traherne's poems cited are from this edition and will here-after be noted in the text.

[3]Christian Ethicks (1675), ed. Carol L. Marks and George R. Guffey (Ithaca: Cornell Univ. Press, 1968), p. 4. All page references to Christian Ethicks (CE) are to this edition and will hereafter be cited in the text.

[4]The Expanded Voice: The Art of Thomas Traherne (San Marino: The Huntington Library, 1970), pp. 14-15.

[5]There has been some critical controversy about Traherne's ortho-doxy. K.W. Salter in Thomas Traherne, Mystic and Poet (London: Butler

& Tanner, 1964), p. 133, has claimed that Traherne inclined to the Pelagian heresy. However, George R. Guffey, questioning the accuracy of some of Salter's evidence and referring to Traherne's discussions in Christian Ethicks, refuted Salter's theory, upholding Traherne's orthodoxy ("Thomas Traherne on Original Sin," N&Q, 14 (1967) 98-100. In addition, A.L. Clements, in The Mystical Poetry of Thomas Traherne (Cambridge, Mass.: Harvard Univ. Press, 1969), has concluded that "Traherne's position, rather than being Pelagian, is much closer to the Anglican doctrine of Original Sin, which is interpreted to mean that human nature is corrupt insofar as it possesses a tendency . . . to evil" (pp. 86-87).

[6]Stewart, p. 146.

[7]The Development of Personality, trans. R.F.C. Hull (New York: Pantheon Books, 1954), p. 41.

[8]M. Esther Harding, The 'I' and the 'Not I': A Study in the Development of Consciousness (Princeton: Princeton Univ. Press, 1965), p. 9. See also George Mead, Mind, Self and Society (Chicago: Univ. of Chicago Press, 1962), p. 172.

[9]Claude Merleau-Ponty, The Structure of Behaviour, trans. Allen L. Fisher (London: Methuen, 1965), p. 167.

[10]Sigmund Freud, The Interpretation of Dreams in The Basic Writings of Sigmund Freud, trans. and ed. A.A. Brill (New York: Modern Library, 1938), p. 294.

[11]Norman O. Brown, Life Against Death (Middleton, Conn: Wesleyan Univ. Press, 1959), p. 26.   Jean Piaget relates in The Language and Thought of the Child, trans. Marjorie and Ruth Gabain (London: Routledge & Kegan Paul, 1959), that the child is not "clearly conscious of intentions contrary to its own" until about the age of three when he "takes cognizance of the resistance set up by things and people," recognizing "a discord between desire and its realization" (pp. 232-233).

[12]Harding, pp. 49-50.

[13]Jung, p. 44.

[14]William James, The Varieties of Religious Experience (New York: Modern Library, 1902), p. 167. See also M. Esther Harding, Journey Into Self (New York: Longmans Green, 1956), p. 27 ff.

[15]Meditations on the Six Days of the Creation (1717) Intro. George Robert Guffey. Augustan Repr. Soc. Pub. No. 119 (Los Angeles: William Andrews Clark Memorial Library, 1966), p. 34. All quotations from the Meditations are from this edition and will hereafter be cited in the text.

[16]The Poetry of Meditation (New Haven: Yale Univ. Press, 1954), pp. 147-48.

[17]The Saints Everlasting Rest (London, 1650), p. 609.

[18]From Silex Scintillans (1655) in The Works of Henry Vaughan, ed. L.C. Martin (Oxford: Clarendon Press, 1957).

CHAPTER VII

JOHN MILTON:
THE FOUR ESTATES IN
PARADISE LOST

Unlike his contemporary, Thomas Traherne, who emphasized the States of Innocence and Grace in order to lead people to conversion by "the Gentle Ways of Peace and Lov,"[1] John Milton focused on the darker side of the picture, dwelling throughout his works on the subjects of sin and temptation. His early masque, Comus, depicts the plight of a young virgin, lost in darkness and subjected to the temptations of pagan sensuality. Areopagitica, his treatise against censorship, argues that we must acknowledge evil as a part of this our fallen world and learn to recognize it in all its forms in order to better resist temptation. His closet drama Samson Agonistes protrays one man's struggle with human weakness, doubt and betrayal, and even Paradise Regained, which has as its theme the promised State of Grace, concentrates on Satan's temptation of Christ, giving the devil as great a role in the dialogue as the Redeemer. Not surprisingly, Milton's monumental epic, Paradise Lost, deals with "Mans First Disobedience"[2] and its fruits, focusing more on the ramifications of the State of Misery than on man's brief sojourn in Paradise. Throughout the poem he unmasks for his readers the many faces of pride, the primal sin and the constant temptations of this world. Revealing to them the insidious disguises and dangers of pride or self-love, which only perpetuates their bondage in the State of Misery, Milton offers his readers a redefinition of heroism in Christian terms, revealing to them the way of unselfish love which leads to their salvation in the State of Grace.

Beginning with the fall of Satan and his followers, Milton introduces the pattern of temptation and disobedience that is echoed in other falls throughout the poem. As Frank Kermode has pointed out, Milton organized his epic so that we would perceive the events in this order: "The Fall from heaven, the Fall from Paradise, and finally the effect of the Fall in the life of humanity in general" in the manner of an Ignatian meditation.[3] And, according to Stanley Fish, a reading of this poem involves the fall of the unsuspecting reader as well.[4] The contrapuntal arrangement of the many falls into the State of Misery in Paradise Lost underscores Milton's didactic purpose: to reveal to his readers the many guises of sin.

The plot itself centers on the parallel falls of the rebel angels and

mankind, which occasion God's monumental plan of justice and mercy.
Both falls are brought about by disobedience, which results from a defi-
ciency in loving, a choice of prideful cupiditas over caritas, and in both
cases the offenders are banished from an initial "happy state" (I.141, I.29)
and hurled into the State of Misery. However, the differences between
these two falls are as significant as their similarities. The first act of
disobedience ends in justice, the second in mercy as Milton's "God" announces:

> The first sort by thir own suggestion fell,
> Self-tempted, self-deprav'd: Man falls deceiv'd
> By the other first: Man therefore shall find grace,
> The other none.

(III.129-32)

Because they fall of their own accord and from the heights of Heaven
itself, there can be no redemption for the fallen angels. They are cast
into the State of Misery and left there for all eternity to suffer God's
wrath under the justice of the old law, while their human counterparts
may partake of God's mercy, which extends to them the possibility of
Grace in this life and the promise of eternal Glory in the next. These,
then, are the basic differences. But let us consider the two parallel falls
individually in order to understand more fully Milton's view of the Four
Estates.

The First Cycle: Diabolical Disobedience

1. Sin: non serviam

As Milton explained in these lines, Satan's

> Pride
> Had cast him out from Heav'n, with all his Host
> Of Rebel Angels, by whose aid aspiring
> To set himself in Glory above his Peers,
> He trusted to have equal'd the most High.

(I.34-40)

For Milton, the primal sin was pride, an egotistical separation from God
and open defiance of his will. This arrogant denial of the One, the unity
behind all things, resulted in the dualism of good and evil where there had
previously been only good, divided the creature from the creator, and
brought discord into the universe. Milton's concept of sin here differs
markedly from that of Traherne. As we have seen, for Traherne, who
virtually ignored the devil in his discussion of evil, sin was essentially a
mistake, a result of misapprehension and a confusion of values. As he
said in Christian Ethicks, "Sin came in [to the world] by the Accidental
abuse of the Creature's Liberty," by Eve's mistake and "Adam's fondness

100

to please his wife,"[5] which made them overlook their primal loyalty to God. The sins of fallen mankind were for Traherne similar to those of their first parents, sins of misapprehension: "Being Corrupt in their Understandings, they are narrow and base and servile in their Affections. They start at a shadow, and boggle at a feather. Sin hath transformed them into slaves and Cowards" (CE, p. 85). Their corrupt understanding makes people hoard their few trinkets and coins and forget that as children of God they possess the whole world and the infinite treasures of the seas and stars.[6] Sin as Traherne described it seems more like a child's foolish mistake than the willful rebellion of a creature who puts himself before his creator.

Milton, however, condemned Satan and all sinners after him as prideful, rebellious, and selfish ingrates who stubbornly put their own will before God's. For Milton, sin was no mistaken apprehension but a conscious act of disobedience, a declaration of enmity against the almighty. Sin was rooted in excessive concentration on the ego and the denial of everything that gets in its way. It was idolatry in the worst sense, worshipping oneself and one's own glory in defiance of the creator. In the character of Satan, whose dark and defiant presence dominates the beginning of Paradise Lost, Milton offers a magnificent example of the appeal of such heroic egoism while at the same time warning of its dangers.

Satan's sin arose from his envy at the exaltation of the Son of God as the heir of the Father, a ceremony which was, as Northrop Frye suggests, a test of the angels' obedience similar to what the forbidden tree would later be for man.[7] At this point, God called upon all the heavenly host to affirm their unity, to swear allegiance to the Son as Lord, that they might be "United as one individual Soule/ For ever happie," warning that "him who disobeyes/ Mee disobeyes, breaks union" (V.610-12). But Satan, his ego wounded by the exaltation of someone else above him, refused to comply. Driven by envy and resentment, he chose to "break union," creating discord by pitting his own will against the will of God.

As is evident in Milton's descriptions throughout Paradise Lost, in its original unfallen state all creation was designed to reflect, and in its own way to imitate the glory of god. However, when one confuses himself with the source, "collapsing analogy into identity" and breaking away from God,[8] this imitation becomes idolatry and casts one into the State of Misery. This was St. Augustine's definition of pride: the perversion that arises when a conscious creature becomes more interested in itself than in God. Sin arises, he explained, when instead of reaching out in an expression of caritas, to serve and glorify God, the creature prefers the inward motions of cupiditas, serving his own personal appetites.[9] Such was the case with Satan, once known as Lucifer, the brightest and most beautiful archangel--bright because he reflected the glory of God--who chose rather to adore and serve his own imperfect splendor than to love and serve God. Love became self-love; he refused to serve, preferring to be served, exalting himself above the other angels in blasphemous imitation of his creator and the Son he so envied. In Book IV Satan admitted to himself that God's service was not hard--involving primarily praise and thanksgivings. But, grounded in pride, he had seen this expression of praise as an obligation, a tedious ritual rather than a spontaneous interchange of love with his creator. So in any relationship without love, the expressions of love are resented as odious tasks.

Satan "understood not that a grateful mind/ By owing owes not" but, seeing everything in terms of his own ego, he

> sdained subjection, and thought one step higher
> Would set [him] highest, and in a moment quit
> The debt immense of endless gratitude,
> So burdensome still paying, still to ow.

> (IV.50-56)

Satan saw service to God as a degrading obligation, enforced servitude, as his speech to Abdiel in Book VI reveals:

> I see that most through sloth had rather serve,
> Ministring Spirits, traind up in Feast and Song;
> Such hast thou armd, the Minstrelsie of Heav'n
> Servilitie with freedom to contend.

> (VI.166-69)

Basing his logic upon a false premise, Satan equated service with sloth, rebellion with courage. This conclusion would have been valid if the service had been involuntary servitude, forced upon the angels against their will, making them God's slaves, his fools and minstrels. But Raphael explains in Book V,

> freely we serve,
> Because wee freely love, as in our will
> To love or not; in this we stand or fall.

> (V.538-40)

The angels' service, then, was active, not passive, an affirmation of their love of God, not weak submissive servitude. Yet Satan and the other fallen angels, who all seem to be of a mind,[10] saw this service as only "splendid vassalage" and "servile Pomp." Their prideful attitude is aptly demonstrated in Mammon's speech in hell, where he says that for him reinstatement in heaven, even if possible, would be unbearable. "We ourselves esteem not of that obedience, or love, or gift, which is of force,"[11] Milton had written in Areopagitica, realizing that such gifts lose their meaning when they are not freely and sincerely given and affirming that the attitude of the giver is even more important than the gifts themselves. Throughout Paradise Lost Milton focused on the subjective nature of perception. Like Traherne, he realized how much one's state of mind determines his view of the world, portraying for us the irony of Satan, who affirmed that the mind can create either heaven or hell from the same situation, but who later found himself inwardly in hell even as he stood in the midst of Eden. In Mammon's speech Milton again demonstrates how an individual's prideful egoism can poison for him even heaven itself. Note the heavy sarcasm and obvious resentment with which Mammon describes serving God in heaven, apparently as degrading to him as serving time in prison:

> with what eyes could we
> Stand in his presence humble, and receive
> Strict Laws impos'd, to celebrate his Throne
> With warbl'd Hymns, and to his Godhead sing
> Forc't Halleluiah's; while he Lordly sits
> Our envied Sovran, and his Altar breathes
> Ambrosial Odours and Ambrosial Flowers,
> Our servile offerings. This must be our task
> In Heav'n, this our delight; how wearisom
> Eternity so spent in worship paid
> To whom we hate.

> (II.252, 257, 239-49; italics mine)

The picture is certainly not a happy one and the reader is almost suffocated by the excessive ambrosia, which begins to reek like a heavy perfume, noxious in this case because the praises and offerings would be forced and insincere. The last line says it all: how unbearable an eternity of service "To whom we hate"; how distasteful are the acts of love where there is no love. The selfish prideful attitude of the fallen angels has robbed them of the spontaneous ability to love, making what had once been natural seem forced and artificial and removing all the joy from paradise.

As a clarification of what he meant by service, Milton has provided Abdiel with the final answer to Satan's distorted definition of freedom. "This is servitude," Abdiel explained:

> To serve th'unwise, or him who hath rebell'd
> Against his worthier, as thine now serve thee,
> Thy self not free, but to thy self entrall'd.

> (VI.178-81; italics mine)

Milton indeed equated servitude with bondage, but only when one was forced to serve someone less worthy than himself. This could also include bondage to one's own lower appetites when they debased him and led him away from his highest good. As Stanley Fish acknowledges, throughout Paradise Lost Milton equated freedom with the ability to follow the highest good and very often (as we shall see later with Adam and Eve) freedom within this context meant acknowledging and obeying one's superior. Paradoxically, then, freedom "is obedience because true freedom is the freedom to follow the best, while freedom from God is servitude,"[12] in Satan's case enslavement to his baser passions.

What Satan in his pride sees as freedom is merely his willful rebellion against goodness. "O alienate from God," Abdiel called him, horrified at such a choice (V.877). Satan knowingly elected to cut himself off from his highest good, from the source of creativity and light that had made him "Lucifer," preferring instead to bask in his own limited glory, which was merely an imperfect reflection. His narcissism is represented by the allegorical figure of Sin, who emerged from his own mind. Sin here is essentially idolatry, a worship of his own ego, for Sin was "likest to [Satan] in shape and count'nance bright" (II.756). Preferring to please himself rather than his creator, Lucifer thus recoiled upon this image of himself in almost autoerotic adoration:

> Thy self in me thy perfect image viewing
> Becam'st enamour'd.

$$(\text{II.764-65})$$

Lucifer's infatuation with Sin, like Adam's excessive passion for Eve, is a base imitation of the love of the Father for the Son. However, in each of the two imitations, the lovers, instead of reflecting divine love, cut themselves off from the original by recoiling upon themselves and loving their own images. Furthermore, whereas the holy trinity is the source of all life and creativity, Satan's passion for Sin engenders Death and destruction. There can be no creativity in the State of Misery; when one is cut off from the creative source, he can only destroy. The fallen angels' invention, gunpowder, is itself but an agent of destruction, not "created" but concocted from materials previously extant in heaven. Similarly, Adam's excessive passion for Eve cuts him off from God and completes the act of disobedience that brings death and the State of Misery to this world. Only the Son, who reverses this egoism by denying himself in obedience to God, is able to bring creation out of destruction and good from evil, restoring divine order to mankind by offering them a means of redemption to the States of Grace and Glory. Satan's ironic "The mind is its own place, and in it self/ Can make a Heav'n of Hell, a Hell of Heav'n" (I.254-55) is for him only a half-truth. He has by willful rebellion and destruction made "a Hell of Heav'n" and will soon bring hell to paradise. But only God's creative power can resolve all this evil into a greater good, making "a Heav'n of Hell."

2. Satan: The Heroic Temptation

>   he above the rest
> In shape and gesture proudly eminent
> Stood like a Towr; his form had yet not lost
> All her Original brightness.

$$(\text{I.589-92})$$

As many critics have argued throughout the ages and as this passage readily attests, Satan, even fallen, is an attractive, heroic figure.[13]

Yet this splendid military hero was not glorious to Milton because of his rebellion but because of his "Original brightness," because he had reflected the glory of God. Despite the protestations of Shelley and Blake, the defiant egotism of Satan is not glorified but criticized in Paradise Lost. Milton was not of the devil's party without knowing it. His heroic build-up of Satan's character was much more conscious than that. Because men in the State of Misery are so susceptible to pride, a sin which is "to our unregenerate imaginations . . . very nearly a virtue,"[14] Milton made his Satan the archetype of the proud, defiant hero whom his fallen readers too easily admire for all the wrong reasons. Milton then proceeded to undercut this kind of heroism in order to educate his readers to what he considered true heroism in Christian terms,[15] correcting our initial tendency to admire external heroics and ignore the far more meaningful spiritual struggle. In an important way, Paradise Lost is a redefinition of the epic. In this Christian epic Milton sought to evolve beyond established tradition by first employing traditional themes and concepts and then transcending them.

In his own life Milton seems to have revised his original definition of heroic virtue and Paradise Lost reflects this change. We have Milton's word that he had originally intended to write a national epic based on the Arthurian legend,[16] and one early biographer even hints that Milton himself tried to emulate certain heroic and military virtues: "his gait erect and manly, bespeaking courage and undauntedness . . . on which account he wore a sword while he had his sight, and was skilled in using it."[17] --Perhaps a bit surprising for those of us who can imagine "the Lady of Christ's" wielding nothing heavier than a pen. Nonetheless, in his personal as well as his public life, Milton as a young man appears to have been fascinated by the heroic ideal. His prose documents often seem the literary counterparts of epic challenges and there is no doubt that he believed that in answering Salamasius and the others he was fighting for his country and for the victory of the Puritan cause. Yet the often exciting furor of the civil war which had promised nothing less than the Millennium shortly forthcoming ultimately left Milton old, tired, and blind--for he had given his eyesight in the service of his country--to suffer the return of the cavalier Charles II and the power of the monarchy to England. No wonder, then, that he revised his original plans for a military epic and even satirized this genre, as Arnold Stein suggests,[18] intent on showing that the physical realm to which fallen men are too readily drawn as a measure of virtue is itself an illusion and that the only enduring reality is the far more intangible realm of spiritual fortitude, the "paradise within," greater far than our futile hopes of earthly glory. For he had learned that spiritual glory cannot be gained by armies, not even new model armies, and that heaven itself is ultimately the only glory worth fighting for. Our attraction to heroic figures, famous in terms of this world, is, he realized, inherently dangerous because it distracts us from seeking true virtue and lasting fame in the eyes of God.

As Stanley Fish explains, Satan "exemplifies a form of heroism most of us find easy to admire because it is visible and flamboyant,"[19] and Milton deliberately made his Satan attractive in all the ways that appeal to the ego, the sense of the melodramatic and the fatal tendency to pride in each of us. Helen Gardner notes that Milton's representation of Satan is "intensely dramatic,"[20] appealing at once to our emotions and imagination as such charismatic leaders do in real life. As J.B. Broadbent observes, Satan is not introduced as a villain--that would be too simple--but as an epic hero or the hero of a revenge tragedy.[21] Such a portrayal of Satan is completely in keeping with Milton's realization that in this fallen world good and evil are intertwined "and in so many cunning resemblances hardly to be discerned."[22] Depicted in terms that ring of epic heroism and (unlike the Son and all the good characters) provided with soliloquies which reveal his very soul, Satan draws us to him with an almost irresistible magnetism. Eloquent, intelligent, courageous and dynamic and (at least at first) physically attractive, Satan appeals to the latent pride in each one of us. He tempts us to act out our own melodramas, to exalt ourselves in defiance of all order and morality as surely as dictators have drawn entire nations under their charismatic spells, playing on people's yearning for a sense of importance and drama in their lives. Milton knew only too well the emotional weakness of fallen humanity, which makes us admire flamboyant heroes and brings us under the hypnotic appeal of charismatic leaders.

Like Traherne, Milton also realized our tendency to confuse the appearance of heroism with its reality. His Satan is apparently a hero in the grand epic tradition: valiant, courageous, inexorable. Yet, when cut off from goodness, what is courage but foolhardiness in one situation and sheer ruthlessness in another? In Paradise Lost Milton has rendered dramatically the lesson that Traherne emphasized throughout Christian Ethics: the importance of seeing beyond appearances. Both authors counseled their readers not to be misled by what seems brave or praiseworthy but to make sure that such deeds are motivated by goodness before giving them the name of virtue and admiring those who perform them as heroes. "What is Courage in a Thief, or a Tyrant, or a Traytor, but like Zeal and Learning in a pernicious Heretick," Traherne pointed out, explaining that "Goodness is a principal Ingredient in the excellency of this [or any] Vertue" (CE, p. 164). Courage in a thief, a tyrant, or a traitor--can anyone, even today, admire a courageous act in such a context? The seventeenth century was not an age of romantic rebels and anti-heroes but a time when people were taught to consider a single action in relation to the larger scope of things. Thus, Traherne defined "Valour" as "a right and strong Resolution of the Soul, whereby it dare encounter with any Difficulty and Trouble, for Vertues sake" (CE, p. 161; italics mine). By this contemporary definition, Satan's perilous flight up through hell and chaos was not valiant because it was not performed in the service of virtue, but for the sake of evil--revenge upon God. Very much a man of his time, Milton realized that misguided zeal and misdirected courage, no matter how glorious they seem, are not only inherently wrong, but also insidiously seductive. Hoping to make his readers aware of the difference between true heroism, which leads them to the State of Grace, and its counterfeit, which entangles them more deeply in the State of Misery, Milton focused on this issue throughout Paradise Lost.

Many critics have called attention to the awkwardness of Milton's writing in the scenes involving epic combat and Louis Martz has even seen his stylistic weakness as intentional, a deliberate effort on Milton's part to "attenuate and ridicule the heroic mode."[23] As I see it, not only does his style vary in these scenes, but Milton also employs a rising and falling pattern in his epic descriptions. He builds up and then undercuts his heroes in a concerted effort to educate his readers away from their old habits of thinking and lead them out of the labyrinthine mazes of pride which keep them in the State of Misery. Milton realized that as long as his readers perceived the world in terms of mere physical victories and admired proud charismatic heroes, they would follow these examples, striving for no more than the transient glories of the State of Misery. Only by redefining virtue to them, by showing them repeatedly how spiritual glory outshines the mere physical, could Milton hope to break his readers' addictions to ego-centered heroics and lead them to recognize the virtues of humility and service which are an integral part of the State of Grace.

One fine example of Milton's technique of building up, then undermining his epic heroes occurs in the confrontation between Satan and Michael. The initial description plays on the readers' desire for action, excitement, and even violence:

> The Battel hung; til Satan, who that day
> Prodigious power had shewn, and met in Armes
> No equal

(VI.246-48)

confronted Michael the Archangel. Then they exchange heroic addresses, challenging each other to combat, and we are reminded of similar dramatic confrontations between such well-matched heroes as Coriolanus and Tullus Aufidius. Prepared for another clash of the irresistible force and the immoveable object, we applaud Satan's magnificent defiance as he upholds

> The strife of Glorie: which we mean to win,
> Or turn this Heav'n it self into the Hell
> Thou fablest, here however to dwell free,
> If not to reign: mean while thy utmost force,
> And join him named Almighty to thy aid,
> I flie not, but have sought thee farr and nigh.

(VI.290-95)

But what at first seems the ultimate in hand to hand combat is undercut by the subtle fact that Michael's powerful sword, which enables him to wound Satan has been provided by God; thus, God is in control here, not the angels themselves. Moreover, this dramatic confrontation has resolved nothing, for Satan's wound is only temporary.

It is not skill at swordsmanship or military might that will win the battle of good against evil. Milton makes this point in another, more frustrating showdown in Book IV, where he uses his epic voice to promise us another exciting clash, this time between the heroic figures of Satan and Gabriel, who exchange threats and prepare for combat. Here again Milton builds his description to a dramatic climax:

> th'Angelic Squadron bright
> Turnd fierie red, sharpning in mooned hornes,
> Thir Phalanx, and began to hemm him round
> With ported Spears, as thick as when a field
> of Ceres ripe for harvest waving bends
> Her bearded Grove of ears, which way the wind
> Swayes them.
>
> (IV.977-83)

Surrounded by an army of enemy angels, their spears hemming him in on all sides, even Satan is "alarmed," but he fiercely stands up to his full height:

> Collecting all his might dilated stood,
> Like Teneriffe or Atlas unremovd:
> His stature reached the Skie, and on his Crest
> Sat horror Plum'd; nor wanted in his graspe
> What seemd both Spear and Shield.
>
> (IV.985-90)

But then after all this buildup, Milton deprives his readers of the promised battle, telling us that

> now dreadful deeds
> Might have ensu'd, nor onely Paradise
> In this commotion, but the Starrie Cope
> Of Heav'n perhaps, or all the Elements
> At least had gon to rack, disturbd and torne
> With violence of this conflict.
>
> (IV.990-95)

had not God at this point hung his scales of judgement in the sky, weighing Satan's might, now cut off from the source of life, as less than Gabriel's. After this divine intervention, Gabriel replies:

> Satan, I know thy strength, and thou knowst mine,
> Neither our own but giv'n; what follie then
> To boast what Arms can doe, since thine no more
> Than Heav'n permits, nor mine.
>
> (IV.1006-09)

Here Milton not only frustrates his readers' desire for the excitement and violence of epic combat, but also declares that combat virtually meaningless, for all combatants fight not with their own might but with only as much as "Heav'n permits." Thus, all the battles that are won and lost are decided not by the valor of the contestants alone, but ultimately by the will of God.[24]

If Milton shows us the futility of single combat, the emptiness beneath the heroic and chivalric ritual, his description of the war in heaven offers ample testimony of his belief that whole armies fare no better. Great was the warfare in heaven, he tells us, great at least in terms of the noise it generated:

> now storming furie rose,
> And clamour such as heard in Heav'n till now
> Was never, Arms on Armour clashing brayd
> Horrible discord, and the madding Wheeles
> Of brazen Chariots rag'd; dire was the noise
> Of conflict.

$$(VI.207-12)$$

But as Milton presents it, all this sound and fury ultimately signifies nothing. After two days of furious fighting with the two armies finally throwing mountains at each other in what Arnold Stein has seen as "mock-epic" exaggeration,[25] still nothing is resolved until God finally calls out the Son to finish the battle by driving Satan's forces out of heaven.

In a manner unusual for an epic, Paradise Lost reflects Milton's very strong anti-war sentiment.[26] A passage in Book II, for example, terms human aggressors worse than devils, for they at least can maintain concord in hell, while "God proclaiming peace," men and women

> Yet live in hatred, enmity, and strife
> Among themselves, and levie cruel warres,
> Wasting the Earth, each other to destroy.

$$(499-502)$$

Hence, his recurrent undercutting of the heroic facade of war, which, however well fought and with whatever glorious ideals, can only result in destruction and cannot win the only fight worth winning: the spiritual battle of good and evil. One is reminded of the passage in Matthew 26:51-54 in which when a disciple takes out his sword and strikes a servant of the high priest, Christ reproves him with: "Put up againe thy sword into his place: for all they that take the sword, shall perish with the sword. Thinkest thou that I cannot now pray to my Father, and he shall presently give mee more then twelve Legions of Angels? But how then shall the Scriptures be fulfilled?"[27] It is clear in Paradise Lost that Milton abjured the way of the sword, repeatedly demonstrating that this was not the way to fulfill the Scriptures and bring about the promised State of Grace.

It is the Son who ultimately ends the battle of good and evil angels in heaven, resolving the discord wrought by sin not with the sword but with the power of God. As the Father tells him, the angels could go on fighting this war forever, for "none but Thou/ Can end it" (VI.702-03). In his role as divine judge, the Son, according to Milton, executes the Father's will:

> in Mercy and Justice both,
> Through Heav'n and Earth, so shall my glorie excel,
> But Mercy first and last shall brightest shine.

(III.132-34)

As Milton shows us in <u>Paradise Lost,</u> only the Son can bring about this victory over evil, administering justice to the apostates by driving them out of heaven like a herd of goats. The good angels stand to the side; they have done their best, but without the aid of the Messiah the service of man or angel alone is ineffectual against sin. Here Milton makes his point about the respective importance of faith and works, while the Son overcomes the fallen angels not by epic combat, but with a chariot that blazes with the awesome power of God.

In the later books, the Son begins the second part of his role as divine judge, tempering justice with mercy toward fallen mankind, his love redeeming them from evil in a combat that, like his kingdom, is "not of this world." Whatever deviations historical Christianity has made from Milton's time to our own, the Christian tradition repeatedly affirms that one cannot overcome evil with evil, but only with the power of divine love. Thus, the disciples were told to "turn the other cheek" and Christ overcame Adam and Eve's wilful disobedience with willing obedience and loving self-sacrifice. Such is the role of the Son as Milton portrays him in <u>Paradise Lost</u> and even further in <u>Paradise Regained</u>, fighting "the better fight" and demonstrating "the better fortitude" (IX.29) of Christian heroism, which brings the State of Grace to mankind and provides us all with a new model of virtue and courage.

Against the Son and the many "types of Christ" who foreshadow his heroic obedience and love, Milton opposes not only the misdirected valor of the fallen angels, but also the ineffectual military efforts of the heavenly host (ineffectual, because, as we have seen, only the power of God, not good works alone, can overcome evil). He holds out to his readers the Limbo of Vanity, an example of the wrong kind of fame, the vanity of resting in the glory of this world. Here Milton offers a lesson to "all who in vain things/ Built thir fond hopes of Glorie or lasting fame . . . Naught seeking but the praise of men" (III.448-50, 453). The glory and physical victories of this world, he affirms, are mutable at best and are ultimately irrelevant to one's salvation. Wars may be won and lost, kingdoms may rise and fall and be restored, as Milton realized, but the only true fame, the only fame that really counts, is heavenly. He had learned when he wrote "Lycidas" as a young man (and he realized even more in later life) that "<u>Fame</u> is no plant that grows on mortal soil."[28]

Through his suffering and disappointments, Milton had developed his own definition of heroic virtue, changing his earlier plans for an Arthurian epic (Warrs, hitherto the only Argument/ Heroic deem'd, chief maistrie to dissect/ With long and tedious havoc fabl'd Knights/ In battels feign'd) to those of a "better fortitude/ Of Patience and Heroic Martyrdom" (IX.26-30). He realized that ultimately the greatest victory one can achieve is, like Abdiel, to merit the divine approval of "Servant of God, well done" (VI.29), and it is this model he develops with progressive emphasis throughout <u>Paradise Lost</u>. Milton's epic may open with the attractive and all-too-familiar figure of the epic hero, but Satan's grandeur diminishes and even his best qualities become obsolete as we are gradually introduced to a new concept of heroism, beginning with Abdiel and concluding in the last two books with a vast panorama of all the false heroes contrasted with all the virtuous individuals, finally culminating with the Son in his role as Messiah, who overcomes disobedience with obedience, self-love with divine love, and eternal Misery with the States of Grace and Glory.

3. The State of Misery: the "darkness visible" of Hell

The State of Misery, the punishment for sin, was for Milton an extension of sin itself: the prideful separation of the individual from God and thus all goodness, beauty, and divine order. In his pride Satan had preferred to serve himself before God and had solipsistically denied his own creation, merely because he could not remember it, making ego alone the measure of all that exists and taking nothing on faith (with the same argument most of us could deny our own births).[29] He arrogantly asked Abdiel:

> rememberst thou
> Thy making, while the Maker gave thee being?
> We know no time when we were not as now;
> Know none before us, self-begot, self-raisd
> By our own quick'ning power.

> (V.857-61)

Claiming total self-sufficiency, Satan denied his need for God:

> Our puissance is our own, our own right hand
> Shall teach us highest deeds, by proof to try
> Who is our equal.

> (V.864-67)

Thus, he cut himself off from the source of his own beauty and power, bringing imperfection upon himself as the earliest evidence of his fall into Misery. The angels in heaven, sustained by their union with God, remained invulnerable to all injury. But the apostate angels, by willfully cutting themselves off from the source of all goodness, became susceptible to evil, experiencing pain and physical injury. As Satan soon realized and Nisroch complained,

> Sense of pleasure we may well
> Spare out of life perhaps, and not repine,
> But live content, which is the calmest life:
> But pain is perfet miserie, the worst
> Of evils, and excessive, overturnes
> All patience.

(VI.459-64)

As we shall see later, pain and suffering also enter the once-perfect world of Adam and Eve when they fall from Innocence to Misery, departing from obedient oneness with God to disobedience and death. In each case, "pain is perfet miserie," destroying the healthful harmony of either man or angel. It is the inevitable consequence of preferring imperfection to perfection and oneself to God.

But pain is not the only evidence of one's fall into the State of Misery. Another consequence of the loss of perfection is the loss of prelapsarian beauty. Adam and Eve's perfect bodies are, from the moment of their fall, subjected to the mutability of the aging process, injury, the possibility of disease, and finally death itself.[30] Similarly, the apostacy of Lucifer and his host dims their formerly dazzling beauty into a mere shadow of what it had been in heaven. "If thou beest he; but O how fall'n! how chang'd" (I.84), says Satan to Beelzebub in hell, realizing how much his comrade's former "transcendent brightness" has faded with his disobedience (I.86). The angels' beauty, like that of their earthly counterparts, was only a reflection of the glory of God and when Satan and his crew rejected God, who is light and beauty itself, there remained for them only the "darkness visible" (I.63) of hell and their own imperfect strength and lustre.

As we have seen, for Milton the State of Misery brought a similar exposure to pain and physical degeneration for both the fallen angels and fallen mankind. However, there are some important differences in the historical State of Misery as it involves these two groups in Paradise Lost. One major difference lies in the effect of the two falls upon order and degree. As Renaissance writers were fond of reiterating, the disobedience of Adam and Eve brought mutability to their world, resulting in disorder and continual change in everything beneath the sphere of the moon. This microcosmic and macrocosmic imbalance caused the extremes of weather, and the physical and emotional imbalances in human beings which resulted in diseases within them and discord among them so that they found themselves assailed by storms on all sides. As Milton explains in Paradise Lost, because the chain of order was weakened when Adam and Eve disobeyed their creator, everything beneath them on the chain was subject to disorder. The animals, which had once played together, loved and respected our first parents, and eaten only vegetation, became wild after the fall, devouring each other in carnivorous frenzy and running from human beings with a new fear and hostility.

112

However, this extensive loss of order which afflicts Adam and Eve and their world is not experienced by the fallen angels. As we can clearly see from an examination of Pandemonium and Satan's empire in hell, the fallen angels still retain a framework of order. Although they cut themselves off from God, the source of all true order, they observe rank and decorum in hell and remain loyal and obedient to their leader, Satan. This is apparent in our first glimpse of the infernal legions, when Satan calls them together. They lie entranced, scattered like "the Autumnal Leaves that strow the Brooks/ In Vallombrosa" (I.302-03). Yet their disoriented state is soon overcome by their loyalty to their leader: "to thir Generals Voyce they soon obeyd" (I.337), lining up in their ranks on the brimstone. Later Satan sits high on his throne in Pandemonium, an ornate capitol constructed by the fallen angels, and they conduct their council, again observing proper degree and ceremony.

Although Eve attempts to upset the established "political" order on earth by rebelling against Adam's authority, there is no such conspiracy in hell. Satan explains this lack of competitiveness in hell by contrasting it to "The happier state/ In Heav'n," which "might draw/ Envy from each inferior" (II.24-26). In heaven, where order is based on ascending degrees of goodness, one may well covet a higher place, he says,[31] but not in hell, where no good exists to arouse envy and competitiveness:

> where there is then no good
> For which to strive, no strife can grow up there
> From Faction.

(II.30-32)

Indeed, Satan argues that his high rank in hell only exposes him to more evil: "greatest share/ Of endless pain?" and makes him a prime target for "the Thunderers aim" (II.29-30, 28). Satan's explanation may of course be seen as a political speech, designed to insure his continued reign in hell, but the fact remains that his followers do not even attempt to rebel. And perhaps he has pointed out why. On earth where there still exists the possibility of greater good, human beings are driven, often intoxicated by that possibility, using any means to achieve their confused perceptions of the highest glory. But bereft of all possibility of good, the fallen angels become stoics, settling for a kind of grim contentment with their lot in hell, which they cannot strive to improve except with Mammon's superficial comforts. They turn instead to the resolution of despair; dismissing all hopes of improving their condition, they choose instead to expend all their efforts on revenge against the almighty.

Like their fallen earthly counterparts, Satan and his crew experience the inner storms of disordered passions, but in hell these do not affect the pyramid of order and degree. As we have seen, there is a definite difference in the external aspects of the State of Misery for these two groups. Perhaps another explanation for this difference can be found in Milton's use of an extended emblem or conceit in Paradise Lost to achieve his artistic purpose: portraying for his readers "the ways of God"

113

and contrasting them with the ways of the devil. As an artist, Milton worked symbolically in the early books of Paradise Lost, constructing two opposing forms of light and darkness to emphasize the difference between good and evil, depicting hell as a diabolical parody of the true order of heaven. The divine order, grounded on obedience to God, approaches the creator by ascending levels of goodness. The infernal order, an inversion of the true, is grounded on prideful disobedience of the creator and its highest ranks, as Satan has pointed out, only appear to ascend, but actually descend in the direction of further Misery. Hell has its unholy trinity of Satan, Sin, and Death, which parodies the heavenly trinity of Father, Son, and Holy Spirit. In every sense, it would seem, is hell an inverse parody of heaven with the devils' pride the reverse of the angels' humility, the darkness of hell the reverse of the radiance of heaven. Milton has presented the State of Misery of the fallen angels almost in the manner of a landscape artist. The inverted order in hell mirrors the true order in heaven just as the glorious natural beauty of a mountain might be reflected in the waters of a murky lake: inverted and obscured. Thus, Milton has constructed for his readers a dramatic emblem of the opposition of heavenly love and its baser reflection, self-love or pride, the two polarities of loving which either damn one to the State of Misery or redeem him to the State of Grace and eternal Glory, two opposing forces which Milton stresses in one way or another, throughout Paradise Lost.

Another major difference between the historical State of Misery for the fallen angels and that of their earthly counterparts is, of course, its duration. For human souls, the State of Misery may be succeeded by redemption to the States of Grace and Glory, but for the fallen angels there is no such relief: they are eternally damned. Many theological writers have dwelled on this difference, seeking to explain it, most of them citing the difference in the degree of the offense. Thomas Traherne, for example, pointed out that because the angels were initially placed in a higher state than Adam and Eve, they were therefore more culpable for falling:

> The Angels were placed in such an Estate, that if they
> fell, it would be with more shame; yet if they stood, it
> would be with less Glory: For having the Advantages of
> Greater Light and strength, to Sin against them was more
> Odious, and to stand in them less Wonderful. While man,
> being more remote from God, was more Obnoxious to
> Dangers, and more Weak to resist them; His want of clear
> Light if he fell, would lessen his offence; And the Diffi-
> culties wherewith he was surrounded, if he stood, would
> increase his Vertue, which by consequence would make
> his Obedience more pleasing, and much augment his Eter-
> nal Glory. All which put together, when Angels and Men
> both fell, fitted Man rather to be chosen and redeemed;
> he being the Greater Object of Compassion and Mercy.

> (CE, p. 104)

114

While Milton's "God" explains the difference in punishment with the fact that the angels fell "Self-tempted, self-deprav'd," whereas Adam and Eve fell "deceiv'd/ By the other" (III.130-31), Milton also seems to share Traherne's view of the difference of their initial estates. In Paradise Lost we learn that the fallen angels were originally in union with God in heaven; thus, they fell from Glory, the highest of the four estates. And although Milton often parallels the fall of the angels and humanity, he makes it clear that the angels have never at any time been in a State of Innocence. For one thing, as we can see from their dialogues with Adam, the angels know too much to be accounted innocent. Raphael and later Michael reveal their wealth of knowledge about God and the universe in their visits to Adam, whose paucity of knowledge puts him in a state far inferior to theirs. The fact that Satan and his host fell with their angelic intellects and greater knowledge makes their offense inexcusable. So also does the fact that the apostate angels fell from heaven itself and union with their creator. To what higher estate could they be redeemed, if indeed they were worthy of redemption? Having fallen from the highest state, they obviously do not have the ability to remain loyal, even in heaven and would most probably fall again, as Satan himself admits. Unlike human souls, they cannot learn through their suffering in Misery and untimately merit redemption to a higher state. There is no higher state than Glory and the devils are despicable because they have failed to remain good even there. Thus, for them there is no alternative but eternal damnation.

But this raises another question in this poem which Milton leaves unanswered. The State of Glory to which man will ultimately be redeemed is generally regarded as a state of eternal bliss in which he will be blessed with perfect union with his creator and spared further temptation and possibility of sin. So Milton portrays it in Michael's speech to Adam in Book XII, at which Adam rejoices, "O goodness infinite, goodness immense!" (469). But a troublesome point is that this State of Glory appears to be the very state from which the apostate angels fell. If this is so, one wonders if the State of Glory as Milton portrays it is really a state of absolute perfection for human souls, or if they will be able to fall, even here. Certainly, the good angels who remain in Glory are free to fall, for Milton felt that to deprive them of this potential would be to make them God's slaves, not his servants. Their free will is apparent in Raphael's advice to Adam in Book V:

> My self and all th'Angelic Host that stand
> In sight of God enthron'd, our happie state
> Hold, as you yours, while our obedience holds;
> On other surety none; freely we serve,
> Because wee freely love, as in our will
> To love or not; in this we stand or fall.

(535-40)

Thus, if in Paradise Lost the angels are still free to fall from Glory, even after the initial apostacy, can we not also see this as a possibility for human beings? But in Books XI and XII Milton portrays the State of Glory for humanity as an apocalyptic consummation of all of their trials and suffering on earth. It is apparently the last chapter in the evolution of the individual through the Four Estates, the ultimate reward for all the faithful. The sense of an ending, of Glory as the goal of perfection for all those who, like Adam and Eve, wander in this postlapsarian world is very strongly conveyed in Paradise Lost. For without a final reward in Bliss with no possibility of another relapse into sin, human life would seem like an eternal treadmill. Milton never resolved the theological contradiction in the poem, but managed to distract his readers' attention to a great degree by his structural artistry. The momentum builds in the last books with Michael's lecture which spans the whole of human history as a prelude to the birth of Christ, the promised redeemer, who returns to us the grace of God. This culminates in a description of the second coming, in which Christ will appear:

> In glory of the Father, to dissolve
> Satan with his perverted World, then raise
> From the conflagrant mass, purg'd and refin'd
> New Heav'ns, new Earth, Ages of endless date
> Founded in righteousness and peace and love
> To bring forth fruits Joy and eternal Bliss.

(546-51)

This passage on the end of all earthly time comes at the end of Michael's speech and very near the end of Paradise Lost itself, all of which combines to give a sense of an ending and finality to the State of Glory as well. Seen in this context, this ultimate state is the promised consummation of the union of God and mankind that sustains all Christians as they face the trials of this world. And moved along by Milton's artistry, the average reader has probably forgotten that until they are redeemed to the "New Heav'ns, new Earth" of the historical State of Glory, the individual State of Glory they will experience after death is presumably the same one from which Satan fell, initiating the entire drama of the Four Estates. That the potential to fall still exists in heaven for the angels and perhaps even themselves is a possibility that Milton obviously did not want his readers to consider.

4. The State of Misery for the Individual:
"My self am Hell"

If Milton presents us with theological inconsistencies in his portrayal of the historical State of Misery, such is not the case for the individual state. For humans and angels alike, Misery can be equated with pride and alienation. Satan's pride is apparent in his blind egotism which leads him to rejoice, even in hell, because he believes himself at last free of dependence on God's will. Defiantly he exults:

To reign is worth ambition though in Hell:
Better to reign in Hell, than serve in Heav'n.

(I.262-63)

But he is wrong; his rebellion against God has put him in the unenviable
position of serving against his will in hell instead of freely serving in
heaven. While in heaven his service was truly voluntary, now he is being
"used" by God to further the divine plan, serving only to bring greater
good out of evil. How much better to have chosen the freedom of obedience: better service in heaven than servitude in hell. For Milton repeatedly shows us that "all acts are performed in God's service; what is
left to any agent is a choice between service freely rendered and service
exacted against his will. Satan continually deludes himself by supposing
that he can act apart from God."[32] In Book I, Satan and Beelzebub, still
misguided, rise from the burning lake:

Both glorying to have scap't the <u>Stygian</u> flood
As Gods, and by thir own recover'd strength,
Not by the sufferance of supernal Power,

(I.239-41)

although Milton explicitly tells us that they rose only through "the will/
And high permission of all-ruling Heaven" (I.211-12). Even in hell, the
power of God is supreme; but the devils, blinded by their original solips-
ism, the pride that had cut them off from God, can see no further than
themselves. This narrow view is reflected even in their choice of recrea-
tion. After the assembly in hell, we learn that in their songs the fallen
angels boast of themselves like so many would-be Beowulfs:

With notes Angelical to many a Harp
Thir own Heroic deeds and hapless fall
By doom of Battel; and complain that Fate
Free Vertue should enthrall to Force or Chance.

(II.548-51)

Although they sing "with notes Angelical" they boast of themselves, of
"Thir own Heroic deeds," while the unfallen angels look beyond themselves,
singing hymns of praise or thanksgiving to God. Again, we see that sin
has resulted in the bondage of egotism and pride, as the fallen angels can
only dwell on themselves and complain of their fate, even in song.

But Milton gives his readers their greatest insight into the State of
Misery for the individual in his description of Satan, who has forever
maimed himself psychologically by turning from <u>caritas</u> to <u>cupiditas</u>. As
Helen Gardner points out, at the beginning of the poem he seems to have
everything--beauty, strength, heroic grandeur--everything, that is, except
"the power to love, . . . to wish good to another being than himself."[33]
It is this inability to love which is his greatest source of misery, even in

117

paradise, the hell within him that forever torments Satan with bitterness and envy. As C.A. Patrides has explained, "Love is centrifugal, pride centripetal"[34]: love reaches outward expressively, creatively; pride reaches inward to the self in self-aggrandizement and satisfaction of the appetites. Originally, God and all creation had expressed themselves in an interchange of divine love: God giving to the angels, who returned the favor in songs of praise, freely given. But by recoiling upon himself in narcissistic adoration, thus giving birth to "Sin," Satan had broken the flow of creative energies and reversed the direction of his love so that instead of desiring to glorify God, he preferred to gratify himself. Such an attitude gives rise to competitiveness and envy. Instead of enjoying all creation as one and leading to the greater glory of God, he began to see himself apart from the whole, and to resent others for having something he wanted for himself. Thus, he envied the Son, recognizing his glory as good but unable to celebrate it and thereby unite with it because he perceived himself as a separate entity. His inability to love anyone but himself is also apparent later, as he views Adam and Eve, whose beauty and goodness he feels himself drawn to initially:

> and could love, so lively shines
> In them Divine resemblance, and such grace
> The hand that formd them on thir shape hath pourd.

                          (IV.363-65)

Gifted with an archangel's sensitivity to beauty (for angels were created to perceive and to love the beauty and goodness of God), Satan is yet plagued by his own self-appointed separation from the divine order. Imprisoned within the limited confines of his ego, which will not allow him to love that which is intrinsically loveable unless he can possess it for himself, Satan cannot enjoy the beauty of Adam and Eve:

> aside the Devil turnd
> For envie, yet with jealous leer maligne
> Ey'd them askance, and to himself thus plaind
> 'Sight hateful, sight tormenting! thus these two
> Imparadis't in one anothers arms
> The happier Eden, shall enjoy thir fill
> Of bliss on bliss, while I to Hell am thrust.

                          (IV.502-08)

How unlike the unselfish appreciation of Raphael, who delights in Adam and Eve as reflections of their creator, accepting and enjoying their beauty, not envying it! As Frank Kermode aptly reflects, Satan here "acquires some of the pathos of an old voyeur." Unable to love, he leers in envy at those who can; in Raphael's discussion with Adam, Milton later reveals that the angels in heaven make love but those in hell do not: "the price of warring against omnipotence is impotence."[35]

Growing more and more bitter in his inability to love, realizing that

118

the beauty of Eve, which at first overwhelms him, is "not for him or-
dain'd (IX.470), Satan's jealousy turns to the vindictive anger of one who
claims "If I can't have her, nobody can. . . ." "Save what is in destroying,
other joy/ To me is lost," (IX.478-79) he maintains. Having cut himself
off from God, the source of all creativity, Satan becomes the first vandal
in history, remarking "For onely in destroying I find ease/ To my relent-
less thoughts" (IX.129-30). He exults in his pride to destroy in one day
"What he Almightie styl'd" took six days to create (IX.937). But his fiend-
ish pleasure in vandalizing paradise is small recompense for his loss of
love, peace, and joy. A restless, bitter, delinquent spirit, Satan is condemned to a life of perpetual solitude, imprisoned in his own inner hell of
resentment and envy.

Regardless of Milton's own theological views on the subject, in the
universe of Paradise Lost, it is Satan's excessive pride as much as God's
justice which makes repentance impossible for him. In Book I Satan, bat-
tered but unbowed, maintains "To bow and sue for grace/ . . . that were
low indeed" (I.111-14) and continues to complain about "the Tyranny of
Heav'n" (I.124). In his soliloquy in Book IV Satan, like Claudius in Hamlet,
contemplates repentance but declares that for him the price is too high:

> is there no place
> Left for Repentance, none for Pardon left?
> None left but by submission; and that word
> Disdain forbids me, and my dread of shame
> Among the spirits beneath, whom I seduc'd.

> (IV.79-83)

"Submission," he realized, would wound his pride and, perhaps worse, destroy his reputation among the fallen angels. Thus, his desire for fame
and glory among his peers prevents him from choosing the true glory of
God and asserting the courage of Abdiel, who could uphold the truth even
amid the derision of multitudes. Satan realizes that his vanity is too
strong for such singular courage. Yet the tragedy of his predicament is
that he also realizes he is miserable, and even his external glory as mon-
arch of hell does not compensate for his suffering:

> Under what torments inwardly I groane;
> While they adore me on the Throne of Hell,
> . . .   onely Supream
> In miserie.

> (IV.88-92)

Still, Satan, aware of the "deadly hate" (IV.99) that burns within him, says
that even if he repented to escape his suffering, he would only fall again
--so far removed is he from the ability to love freely. Thus, in Milton's
poetic account, with its constant opposition of pride and divine love, Satan's nature as well as God's justice prevents his repentance. "All hope/
is/ excluded" as much by Satan's inability to accept as by God's failure to

grant it (IV.103-05). His heart hardened against his creator, there is nothing left for Satan but irredeemable dispair."[36]

An intelligent, articulate, and sensitive being, Satan is condemned by his overweening pride to suffer in eternal isolation from the divinity he has rejected. Ultimately, his crime becomes his punishment. The freedom he sought from love and service to his creator brings with it an inability to love, to escape from the limits of his ego. Void of all goodness, love, and peace, Satan is filled instead with envy, hatred, and a desire for revenge, which

> boiles in his tumultuous brest,
> And like a devillish Engine back recoiles
> Upon himself; horror and doubt distract
> His trouble'd thoughts, and from the bottom stirr
> The Hell within him, for within him Hell
> He brings.

> (IV.16-21)

In Adam's first dialogue with God, Milton presents a basic doctrine of the poem: that all of creation is good, but that nothing is complete in and of itself. Adam's first impulse is to reach out in love and thanksgiving to his creator (caritas), and soon thereafter he also expresses a need to reach out in love to one of his own kind. Throughout Paradise Lost Milton acknowledges the need of men and angels for communion with God and a sense of community with their peers. But Satan in his pride has wilfully cut himself off from the rest of the universe. God and his creation he can no longer enjoy but instead envies and lashes out against in destructive fury. Even among the other fallen angels Satan has no peers, for his vain desire to keep up a brave front isolates him from them as well. With all avenues to love and joy cut off, what is there left for the apostate angel but despair and eternal alienation, a prison from which he cannot escape? In Book IV he cries out in the realization that the State of Misery follows him even into paradise:

> Me miserable! Which way shall I flie
> Infinite wrauth, and infinite despaire?
> Which way I flie is Hell; my self am Hell.

> (73-75)

Choosing in his pride to love himself before God, he is condemned forever to suffer the bondage of his own ego; Satan in his fall both originates and epitomizes the State of Misery in alienation from God.

120

The Second Cycle: "Of Man's First Disobedience"

1. The State of Innocence

Drawn from the account in Genesis, the commentators, and his own imagination, Milton's paradise is at first everything that we would expect it to be, yet, characteristically, Milton's emphatic humanism and belief in free will made him deviate from tradition and offer his readers a more dynamic definition of the historical State of Innocence. Like his predecessors, Milton believed that the State of Innocence had involved "a three-fold Paradise: an eternal garden of delight, a perfect body attuned to its harmonious surroundings, and a Paradise of perfections . . . within his soul."[37] Adam and Eve and their garden were perfect in the State of Innocence because they reflected the glory of God. Paradise, which contained "in narrow room Nature's whole wealth" was for Milton "A Heav'n on Earth," the garden of God (IV.207-09). And just as their garden resembles heaven, so also do Milton's Adam and Eve resemble their creator. This resemblance is apparent in our first glimpse of them:

> Two of far nobler shape erect and tall,
> Godlike erect, with native Honour clad
> In naked majestie seemd Lords of all,
> And worthie seemd, for in thir looks Divine
> The image of thir glorious Maker shon.

(IV.288-92; italics mine)

Milton goes on to explain that in Innocence Adam and Eve related to God like obedient children; practising "true filial freedom," they remained reflections of their creator as long as they chose to obey him (IV.294).

Reflecting the perfection and harmony of their creator, Adam and Eve in the State of Innocence were at home with all creation. They felt "no guilty shame" or feelings of inadequacy, and although naked, shunned the sight of neither God nor angel for, as Milton emphasizes, "they thought no ill" (IV.313, 320). Perceiving themselves as one with divine order, they felt no separation, no sense of limitation.

As Raphael explains to Adam, their unity with divine order was an integral part of paradise. His homily on order and degree is, of course, a Renaissance commonplace, an emphatic reference to the importance of degree, the violation of which was "the sin above all sins" that threatened to return creation to chaos.[38] Thus, Raphael attempts to teach Adam and Eve to know themselves as a part of this divine order, to see themselves always in reference to the whole, to recognize their rightful part in the hierarchy

It is obvious from their physical descriptions that Adam and Eve have different functions within the order of creation:

For contemplation he and valour formd,
For softness shee and sweet attractive Grace,
Hee for God only, shee for God in him.

(IV.297-99)

As James Holly Hanford has explained, the final line in this passage reveals what was to Milton the "natural hierarchy of existence on earth," the "subordination to a natural superior [which] was indeed, the proper law of the whole universe," with woman looking up to man, man looking up to angel, inferior angel looking to superior angel through their ranks, and all ultimately looking up to God.[39] It is the denial of this order of creation and hence of its creator that precipitates the fall of the angels and that of mankind as well.

Milton reminds us there were restrictions even in paradise: Adam and Eve were commanded not to eat of the forbidden fruit. To Milton this one prohibition was exceedingly important. As he explained in Christian Doctrine, "It was necessary that one thing at least should be either forbidden or commanded, and above all something which was in itself neither good nor evil, so that man's obedience might in this way be made evident" (pp. 351-52). This exercise of free will was equally important to Traherne, who held that "To make our selves amiable and beautiful, by the Exercise of our own Power, produces another kind of Beauty and Glory, than if we were compelled to be good by all his preventing Power. All Goodness is spoiled by Compulsion" (CE, p. 31). Both authors emphasized that this prohibition was necessary in order to allow the individual to serve God in some way and thus demonstrate his loyalty. "He had been else a mere artificial Adam, such an Adam as he is in the motions." Milton stated emphatically in Areopagitica. "God therefore left him free, set before him a provoking object, ever almost in his eyes; herein consisted his merit, herein the right of his reward, the praise of his abstinence."[40] This fact Raphael makes clear in his instructions to Adam: "Our voluntary service he requires,/ Not our necessitated" (V.529-30). Our loyalty to God is demonstrated and our happy state maintained by our obedience, for God's service is not performed by conscription but by the free will, the active choice of humans and angels. There is always the possibility of disobedience, of choosing to serve ourselves instead of God, as Raphael again explains, referring to Satan's fall and the dire consequences of "Eternal miserie" (VI.904). Thus, even in the State of Innocence, Adam and Eve are given the right of self-determination.

Some critics, among them E.M.W. Tillyard and A.J.A. Waldock, have concluded that even with the dignity of free will, visits from angels, and all earthly bliss, life in paradise would have constituted "an eternity of boredom."[41] Tillyard, obviously unimpressed with Milton's description of life in Eden which, he felt, denies people any challenge because of its very abundance, held that "Adam and Eve are in the hopeless position of Old Age pensioners enjoying perpetual youth" and that Milton himself could not have abided life in his paradise but would have eaten the apple just to liven things up a bit.[42]

But is life in Milton's paradise really so uneventful and repetitive? Let us examine the garden more carefully. First of all, Milton seems to have taken pains to make his Eden a challenging environment. In fact, J.B. Broadbent has called the great abundance in Eden excessive and anachronistic because the garden simply "should not need pruning and weeding in innocence."[43] Milton has depicted growth and change, then, even in paradise, which would break the monotony of perfection and eliminate at least one cause of boredom. The profuse growth makes Adam and Eve's labor necessary and not merely a token puttering around in their garden. According to Barbara Lewalski, Milton's Paradise Lost constitutes "a redefinition of the State of Innocence which is a very far cry from the stable, serene completeness attributed to that state in myth and traditional theology." Adam and Eve are part of a world that involves "radical growth . . . life steadily increasing in complexity and challenge" but also in perfection. Paradise is not complete without them but requires their civilizing touch to continue the creation begun by God, to evolve from chaos to a greater order.[44] Thus, Eve adorns her bower, tends her special "nursery" of young flowers, and prepares fruit juice and "dulcet creams," tempering nature with the arts of civilization. And this process is expected to continue as their progeny will help them cultivate the garden even more. Similarly, Lewalski maintains, Adam and Eve themselves are part of the growth process and are expected to "perfect themselves through cultivation."[45] As Milton informs us, Adam and Eve have, since their creation, undergone many learning experiences, acquiring a growing knowledge of themselves and their relationship. One such experience after the creation of Eve teaches her that Adam's intellect merits her admiration far more than the beauty of her own reflection.[46]

Furthermore, in Raphael's counsel to Adam, Milton clearly demonstrates his belief that our first parents were in merely the first phase of an ongoing spiritual evolution:

> Your bodies may at last turn all to Spirit,
> Improv'd by tract of time, and wingd ascend
> Ethereal, as wee, or may at choice
> Here or in Heav'nly Paradises dwell;
> If ye be found obedient, and retain
> Unalterably firm his love entire
> Whose progenie you are.

(V.497-503)

As we have seen, Milton depicted the historical State of Innocence not as static perfection but as a dynamic progression, a process of spiritual growth which would ultimately have placed humans next to the angels. He believed with St. Augustine that if there had been no Fall, the human race after multiplying to its full numbers would have been promoted to "that higher felicity which is enjoyed by the most blessed angels."[47] Again, like St. Augustine, Milton emphasized human depravity at birth. He did not, like many of his contemporaries, see any recapitulation of the State of Innocence in the childhood of the individual.

Interestingly enough, the middle and late seventeenth century appears to have unofficially reawakened the Pelagian-Augustinian debate on innocence versus corruption at birth. However, this time the proponents of innocence maintained a significantly low profile to enable them to remain within the latitudinarian boundaries of seventeenth-century Anglicanism. As we have seen, John Earle, Henry Vaughan and Thomas Traherne wrote of the innocent apprehensions of early childhood, apparently believing that the child's inability to perceive sin and corruption temporarily spared him any awareness of their existence and created for him a vision of the world which glowed again in its original edenic perfection. Thus, Traherne wrote in the Centuries: "I knew not that there were any Sins, or Complaints, or Laws. I Dreamed not of Poverties Contentions of Vices. . . . I saw all in the Peace of Eden" (III.2); concluding that "certainly Adam in Paradice had not more sweet and curious Apprehensions of the World, then I when I was a child" (III.1).

Such was hardly the case with Milton, who never once equated his descriptions of the historical State of Innocence in Paradise Lost with any personal recollections of a similar state. Rather, he dwelled at length on "the depravity which all human minds have in common, and their propensity to sin," in Christian Doctrine and elsewhere, firmly upholding his belief in original sin and never excluding infants or young children from an awareness of their sinful nature (p. 389). Citing many cases in which the sins of the parents were visited upon their children, Milton defended the justice of this, arguing that "As for infants, the problem is solved by the consideration that all souls are God's, and that though innocent they were the children of sinful parents, and God saw that they would turn out to be like their parents" (p. 386). Writing from a Puritan perspective which made him acutely aware of human depravity and which stressed the need for regeneration, Milton focused upon the second and third estates of the individual throughout his works. The major portion of Christian Doctrine deals with the different stages in regeneration. Apparently, Milton felt it more advantageous for man to spend his time learning how to enter the State of Grace than looking back to an Eden he had never known.

Whereas the Anglicans tended to see life not in a linear but in a symbolic sense, in which the same lessons were repeated for man on many different levels and nature was a wealth of hieroglyphs, the Puritans conceived of life, and hence the Four Estates, as a linear progression. The Anglican Sir Thomas Browne revelled in life as an intricate pattern of symbolism, wrought with hieroglyphs which recapitualted one truth on many levels. In the Religio Medici, for example, he conceived of birth on three levels: "In that obscure world and womb of our mother, our time is short, computed by the moon, yet longer than the days of many creatures that behold the sun. . . . Entering afterwards upon the scene of the world, we arise up and become another creature, performing the reasonable actions of man and obscurely manifesting that part of divinity in us, but not in complement and perfection till we have once more cast our secundine, that is, this slough of flesh and are delivered into the last World, that ineffable place of Paul, that proper ubi of spirits."[48] Similarly, the Anglican

Traherne saw himself, on the individual level, repeating the historical fall from Innocence to Misery, for as Joan Webber has pointed out, the Anglican "I" incorporated both the individual and mankind.[49] "I offended in an Apple against Him that gave me the whole World," wrote Traherne, seeing himself simultaneously on two levels of time comprehended by the expanded plane of his consciousness (C I.75), while his Puritan counterparts like Bunyan and Milton maintained that it was impossible for an individual, conceived in sin, to participate in any awareness of edenic innocence. In linear time, an individual cannot return to a state concluded before his particular linear progression has begun. For the Puritans, although mankind began in the State of Innocence, the individual man began life in the State of Misery. He could go forward, by the grace of God, to relive the redemption and be transformed from the Old Adam to the New, but he could never know the innocence of Adam and Eve before the Fall because he himself could never be innocent, born as he was into Misery and sin. Thus, there was no individual State of Innocence for Milton and other seventeenth-century Puritans as it was perceived by many seventeenth century Anglicans: a significant difference in their respective apprehensions of the Four Estates.

2. Danger in Paradise: Human Weakness Before the Fall?

Many critics have argued that Milton could not conceive of the State of Innocence, even as an artist, and that he represented Adam and Eve as fallen individuals within the historical State of Innocence. For some critics, Milton's Adam and Eve were flawed from the start, making their Fall inevitable. John M. Patrick's interpretation of Paradise Lost stresses the "fatal weakness" of their passions which "seems infallibly and teleologically designed to turn [them] away from the path of reason" and lead them to their doom.[50] Now certainly, Milton could not have intended to represent Adam and Eve with such an innate depravity because that would have been theologically unsound, amounting to nothing less than God's predestining them to fall, and Milton makes it clear that they were "Sufficient to have stood, though free to fall" (III.99). But whether Milton perhaps unwittingly depicted Adam and Eve as endowed with postlapsarian weaknesses in their prelapsarian state is another matter, which requires our careful consideration of the controversial passages involving Eve's vanity and Adam's uxoriousness.

According to C.A. Patrides, Milton and his contemporaries regarded Eve as "partly fallen before she actually ate the forbidden fruit, already preoccupied with herself to a dangerous degree."[51] The "mirror scene" in Book IV is usually cited as proof of such preoccupation, but is it really? Let us consider the scene more closely. Eve awakens from her creation and, like Adam, her first impulse is to reach out in an expression of love. As Eve herself relates, she went to the lake "with unexperienc't thought" (IV.457); she did not know that the creature she was reaching out to was her own image. Thus, what is usually read as vanity and self-love is actually an imperfect gesture of caritas. She believed she was reaching out to another being, who seemed to return "answering looks/ Of sympathie and love" (IV.464-65). Like all of God's creatures, she was merely manifesting her natural tendency to love, a tendency acknowledged and rightly directed by God, who then led her to Adam. Furthermore, her momentary faltering and impulse to return to the lake when she saw that Adam was "less winning soft" (479) was soon corrected by Adam, whose superior intellectual beauty she learned to admire above her own:

> I yielded, and from that time see
> How beauty is excelld by manly grace
> And wisdom, which alone is truly fair.

(IV.489-91)

As we have seen, then, this experience develops in Eve her ability to love.[52] Instead of magnifying beyond proportion her initial mistake in the mirror experience, it is important to see it in context and remember where it leads.

Eve's dream, occasioned by Satan's nocturnal whisperings, has also led many critics to condemn her, again, without sufficient cause.[53] Since Eve has learned a lesson from the experience with her reflection, it seems unlikely that she would so soon regress, preferring herself as a love-object to Adam. Her conversation with him upon awakening reveals no such change in her attitude but instead affirms her continued love and admiration. Yet John M. Patrick concludes that the Fall is inevitible as soon as Satan has instilled the desire in Eve, basing his argument on "man's passions" which, he says, frequently overcome his reason and "cause him to expend the furious energies of his spirit in 'a waste of shame'," utilizing the description of the passions in Shakespeare's sonnet 129 in his interpretation.[54] However, in so doing, Patrick anachronistically equates Adam's and Eve's prelapsarian passions with the undeniably postlapsarian reason/passion conflict described by Shakespeare, and as Milton points out in Book IX, such an imbalance of passions does not occur until after the Fall to the State of Misery.

Barbara Lewalski is one of the few who do not see Eve's dream as an indication that individually she is fallen and corrupt while still in the historical State of Innocence. Arguing that Milton conceived of the State of Innocence as a dynamic growth process rather than continuous childlike naiveté, Lewalski maintains that the dream could even be another learning experience, for while it creates new tensions within Eve, it also gives her an insight into evil's true nature which "could greatly enhance her ability and her determination to shun the actual experience."[55] Moreover, when considering her dream, we must remember that it did not arise completely from Eve's unconscious, but that Satan was there to plant the thoughts in her mind. Thus, Eve is responsible not so much for the dream itself as for her reactions to it, which I will consider at length, for I feel that they clearly reveal that she remained at this point both individually and historically in the State of Innocence. For example, observe her response within the dream itself when the angelic figure (presumably Satan) eats the forbidden fruit:

126

```
       mee damp horror chil'd
At such bold words voucht with a deed so bold.
```

                              (V.65-66)

Note that she expresses not excitement, not curiosity, but "horror." To continue within the context of the dream, as Stanley Fish so astutely observes, nowhere do we see Eve actually eating the apple. Rather, the action skips from the angel's holding the fruit up to her mouth and Eve's "that I, methought,/ Could not but taste" to "Forthwith up to the Clouds/ With him I flew" (85-87). The angel shoves the fruit right up to her mouth, forcing her to taste it, and then we are told of the supposed effects of the deed but never of the deed itself. Fish accounts for this omission by explaining that here, even in her sleep, "Satan is unable to make Eve go through the motions of disobedience . . . just as hypnotic suggestion cannot induce actions contrary to one's moral code."[56]

The dream may have exposed Eve to evil, but it has not tainted her with it, as her reactions demonstrate. She awakens with a sense of relief "To find this but a dream" (93) and Adam's discourse on psychology also demonstrates his belief that she has resisted evil, which

```
       into the mind of God or Man
May come and go, so unapprov'd, and leave
No spot or blame behind.
```

                              (117-19)

Angels, too, may be exposed to evil thoughts but as long as they do not accept them, converting them into actions, they remain blameless; so Abdiel could listen to Satan's rhetoric but refuse to accept and act upon it. The dream sequence ends with Adam concluding that since merely dreaming of the deed had so horrified Eve, she would be even less inclined to actually perform it. And Eve, comforted by Adam, cries silently, with Adam recognizing her tears

```
       as the gracious signs of sweet remorse
And pious awe, that feard to have offended.
```

                              (V.134-35)

Yet another sign that the dream has not corrupted Eve; her tears, we are to believe, are spontaneous and genuine, for there is no dissimulation in Innocence. If Eve's will had already been infected to seek Godhead, she simply could not cry here out of "fear . . . to have offended" either Adam or God.

Thus, we have considered the evidence of Eve's supposed weakness before the Fall: her vanity. Let us now turn to the more troublesome matter of Adam's excessive passion. As we have seen, the State of Innocence was for Milton a dynamic process in which Adam and Eve were continuously educated in their ability to know, love, and serve God. As Milton reaffirms throughout Paradise Lost, love is the foundation of the universe. Men and angels were given free will to serve out of love, not necessity. They were intended to exchange love with their creator and with one another, to love wisely and well, which involved knowing themselves and their respective positions in the divine plan. As Milton stated in Christian Doctrine, the "Love of God means love which cherishes him above all other objects of affection, and is eager for his glory. . . . Opposed to this is hatred of God. . . . And love of the world or of created things" (p. 657).

From their first moments of life, Adam and Eve were taught to love God, themselves, and one another. However, the newly-created Adam and Eve were in a peculiar situation. Each was provided with a perfect mind, body, and soul with all of its prelapsarian refinements, but was almost completely devoid of experience. For this reason Eve, like a young child, initially mistakes her reflection in the lake for a real person. She simply does not have the experience necessary to enable her to differentiate. By the beginning of Book VIII Adam and Eve, with the aid of God, the angels, and one another, have already acquired a certain amount of practical knowledge. But they must continue to evolve, to accumulate knowledge, often by trial and error.

In their relationship with one another, Adam and Eve like most newlyweds, are still working things out. This situation is further complicated by their lack of experience. Adam may have the mind and body of a man in his prime, age thirty as most commentators agree. But with virtually no previous experience, he has the emotions of an adolescent, with the familiar tendency to overvalue the person he loves. This tendency is not dangerous in itself, for youthful romance can and often does develop into more mature love. It is just that Adam needs to pay attention, to absorb the lessons God and Raphael try to teach him, and not let the intensity of his passion blind him to the right priorities in life. These priorities Adam knew intuitively following his creation: first reaching out in loving adoration of his creator and then seeking another of his own kind to love. He has only to remember this and love wisely, observing divine order. However, for an emotional adolescent this is no easy task, and for this reason God sends Raphael to tutor him.

As we have seen, Adam's initial responses after his creation were correct, and so was the love he felt for Eve, which infused a new sweetness into his heart, inspiring all things with "the spirit of love" (VIII. 474-77). However, as Adam later confesses to Raphael, he finds that her beauty overwhelms him with passion ("Commotion strange"), which renders him "weake/Against the charm of Beauties powerful glance" (531, 532-33). Perhaps her beauty is too strong, he complains, perhaps God has bestowed on her "Too much of Ornament" (538). Adam realizes that she is "inferiour, in the mind/ And inward Faculties" (541-42). And yet what he knows with his highest reason is contradicted by his passionate love for her:

              yet when I approach
Her loveliness, so absolute she seems
       . . .
. . . that what she wills to do or say,
Seems wisest, virtuousest, discreetest, best;
All higher knowledge in her presence falls
Degraded.

                                        (546-52)

Again, it is her beauty--"her loveliness," "so absolute she seems"--that appears to deny what he knows as true. Here he reveals a tendency to let
appearance dictate reality, an errant inclination which elicits Raphael's
immediate reprimand.

        Adam, with a typical young lover's unbounded adoration, has put Eve
on a pedestal, seeing "an awe/ About her as a guard Angelic plac't" (558-
59). Assuming the subjection of a petrarchan lover, he thus degrades himself, causing Raphael to frown and counter Adam's misguided adoration
with the voice of reason. Eve's beauty, Raphael explains, is not excessive:
"Accuse not Nature, she hath don her part;/ Do thou but thine, and be not
diffident/ Of Wisdom" (561-63). Eve's nature is beauty, Adam's is reason,
the angel reminds him, and he must not, in valuing her, undervalue himself.
Furthermore, whereas his beauty is internal, intellectual, and far superior,
the beauty Adam so admires in Eve is only external:

An outside. fair no doubt, and worthy well
Thy cherishing, thy honouring, and thy love,
Not thy subjection.

                                  (568-70; italics mine)

        Raphael's counsel, "oft times nothing profits more/ then self esteem,
grounded on just and right" (571-72) concurs with Milton's discussion of
charity to oneself in Christian Doctrine: "A man's righteousness towards
himself means right reason in self-government and self-control. . . .
[which] includes both the control of one's inner affections, and also the
pursuit of external good and resistance to or endurance of external evil"
(p. 720). "In loving," Raphael tells Adam, he does well, "in passion not"
(588), for in passion he loses the right reason which seeks for him his highest good. Misdirecting his love, he relegates to Eve all goodness and instead of adoring his creator, he worships a lower creature.

        In adoring Eve's beauty for its own sake, Adam is mistaking the part
for the whole, seeing her synecdochically and not as a total personality.
This could lead him to become so distracted by her beauty that he might
fail to recognize what was best for her--a definite disadvantage when it
is his responsibility to care for her and protect her, as we shall see.
Furthermore, by exalting her beauty above his own greater worth, he is
ignoring and debasing his power of reason, which he must not do if he is
to act wisely. Finally, Adam's excessive fixation on Eve's beauty narrows

                                  129

his field of vision, making him likely to forget the primary love and loyalty he owes to his creator, ignoring the order in loving he had learned intuitively at his creation.

The crucial distinction which Raphael makes in his instructions to Adam is between petrarchan and platonic love. The petrarchan mode--idolizing one's beloved above oneself and virtually ignoring God--was for Milton a perversion, a counterfeit of true love, which was platonic, and in which all creation is admired as a reflection of God. The former is the mode Satan uses in his seductive temptation of Eve; the latter is the love of the angels who serve God and love Adam, Eve, and one another as reflections of their creator. In Paradise Lost Milton condemns petrarchan love, portraying it as another Pandemonium, a prideful parody of divine order, grounded not upon love and obedience to the creator, but instead upon the worship of another creature in order to gratify one's appetites.

Excessive and misdirected, such a love leads its subject through a counterfeit of the Christian Four Estates, creating a melodrama which distracts man from his true quest and leads him away from God. This pattern is easily discernible in an examination of some of the legions of Renaissance sonneteers who preceeded Milton. The lover's "State of Innocence" is, of course, the springtime of love when his rapture makes him feel at one with the universe and he rejoices in the paradise he finds in his beloved. The garden imagery--roses, lilies, etc.--often used in Renaissance sonnets to depict the lady's beauty portray her as the garden of Eden itself. In fact, as Stanley Stewart has pointed out, the lover's conception of his lady as a "garden enclosed" is a literary tradition dating back to the Song of Songs.[57] From this initial perception of love, a lover may, of course, go on to court and marry his lady, all in accordance with divine order. However, since the petrarchan lover's passion makes him lose his perspective and his propensity for suffering often makes him choose impossible situations to begin with, he generally spends most of his time in a "State of Misery." Falling from his lady's favor or failing to win her affections he regards as tantamount to the Fall itself. He cries out in agony, wallows in self-pity, or languishes in despair in the dust beneath the pedestal upon which he has placed his highly-idealized lady. Examples of such misery can be found in scores of sonnets from the Petrarchan translations and adaptations of Wyatt and Surrey to Sidney's Astrophel and Stella. Shakespeare's Romeo, in his hopeless love for the lady Rosaline at the beginning of the play, is an archetypal petrarchan lover who cannot sleep at night but takes to his bed all day, doting on his lady and dramatizing his despair with oxymoronic outcries, mixing love with hate, and sweetness with pain. The freezing fires and sweet pain are characteristic outcries of the petrarchan lover, who appears to dote as much on his own suffering as upon his lady herself, more often than not choosing to love "impossible" women whom he can never hope to marry, women above him in social status or already married to other men. At any rate, his "State of Misery" is filled with conceits emphasizing either his baseness in comparison to his idealized lady or focusing upon his own suffering. Religion, war, and a ship tossed in a stormy sea are some familiar conceits with which he addresses his beloved, laments his fate, expostulates on his own unworthiness, or contemplates death, in a parody of the despair which grips a sinner in the throes of the Christian State of Misery.

However, whereas the Christian State of Misery results from man's alienation from God, this counterfeit centers around man's relationship with a fellow mortal, whom he chooses to worship in idolatry, to the detriment of his relationship with his creator. As Robert Burton has so well depicted it in his Anatomy of Melancholy, petrarchan love, or love melancholy, is an aberration, a mental illness which can only be cured with great difficulty, a complete change of lifestyle, prayer, and spiritual guidance to get the unfortunate victim back to a well-ordered soul and sound set of priorities.

Even if the petrarchan lover manages to sue for "Grace," begging his lady to admit him to her favor and somehow succeeding, the merits of his lady's "Grace" are infinitely inferior to the Grace of God and his preoccupation with the former will often interfere with his salvation. If the lover is successful in his courtship, the third petrarchan estate may even lead him to a fourth estate of consummate bliss or complete union with his beloved. Granted, in its original sense, petrarchan love involved worship from afar and was not expected to extend to the point of sexual consummation, for Petrarch attained only inspiration from his Laura, who led him to achieve literary glory. Nevertheless, the extent to which Elizabeth's "maids of honor" were seduced and impregnated by their courtly lovers bears witness to the power (or perhaps the weakness) of the flesh. The Elizabethan court scandals were nothing in comparison to the worldly court of Charles II. During the time that Milton was writing Paradise Lost it seemed that too many men were seeking "bliss" in a physical rather than a spiritual consummation, adoring the beauties of this world to such a dangerous degree that they ignored the glory of God.

As is evident from a close consideration of Paradise Lost, Milton regarded petrarchan love in the same light as epic heroism: not evil in itself but insidiously dangerous because it leads individuals away from God. He realized that love, like courage, is not virtuous in itself but only so when it directs one towards his highest good. Masking pride as a virtue, petrarchan love, like epic heroism, takes one down the path of damnation rather than salvation. Milton recognized "the selfishness and idolatry that sexual love by its nature may easily fall into" in which the lover in idolizing his beloved, places her on a pedestal as an object for his enjoyment, prizing her for the "excitement she provides" instead of seeing her as a person with her own position in the divine plan.[58] Petrarchan love, with its almost masochistic delight in the lover's own suffering, he saw as self-conscious and inherently prideful, focusing in on the lover's own passions and sensations rather than reaching out in an unselfish act of love. Because such a love stimulates man's pride, causes him to serve his own appetites, and separates him from God, Milton condemned it in Paradise Lost, showing how Adam brings about his own fall into sin by not observing right order in loving, or, if you will, by "falling" in love.

Not that love itself was wrong. Milton emphasized again and again in <u>Paradise Lost</u> that the whole universe revolved around love, both the love of God and the love of one's fellow beings. In fact, what Waldock sees as Milton's later "excursus into the mysteries of angelic copulation for which there was no real excuse at all"[59] represents only another effort on Milton's part to underscore the importance of love in the universe and to emphasize the heavenly nature of love wisely directed, the love, which Raphael says "is the scale/ By which to Heav'nly Love thou maist ascend" (591-92). This right order in loving Milton contrasts with pride and carnal passion, the love of one's own pleasure with no heed of the divine order, in the passage where Raphael bluntly tells Adam that he was meant to love in proper perspective, "for which cause/ Among the Beasts no Mate for thee was found" (593-94). This last remark jolts Adam, as it is meant to, and he replies with reason that Eve's beauty delights him not as much as their mutual exchange of love, sense of community and "Union of Mind" (604). Adam then repeats the lesson he has learned: "To love thou blam'st me not, for love thou saist/ Leads up to Heav'n, is both the way and guide" (612-13).

Recognizing the problems inherent in Adam's misguided ardor, Raphael has used proper pedagogical techniques in instructing him to love wisely. He has first identified Adam's error and explained <u>why</u> his petrarchanism was wrong; then he has described for Adam the right order of loving, which involves rightly esteeming oneself and putting the spiritual before the physical. Seeming to have profited from his instruction, Adam repeats his lesson and learns of angelic love as well. What emerges in this dialogue is a vision of the whole universe ordered by degrees of love and a realization of the vital necessity of loving <u>within</u> the appointed order. As Raphael departs, he concludes his lesson by summing up his main point: the priorities Adam must maintain in loving:

> Be strong, live happie, and <u>love, but first of all</u>
> <u>Him whom to love is to obey</u>, and keep
> His great command; take heed least Passion sway
> Thy Judgement to do aught, which else free Will
> Would not admit.
>
> (633-37; italics mine)

As Raphael leaves, Adam seems to have learned his lesson as Eve has apparently learned hers in the previous episodes. But each day brings with it new experiences and challenges. Whether they will apply what they have learned, converting knowledge into wisdom to help them make the best decisions is ultimately up to them. As I see it at this point, they continue so, growing in the knowledge of themselves and their creation if they can only remember these lessons when the need arises.

The next day provides a demonstration not so much of any inherent weakness on the part of Adam and Eve but rather of their failure to apply the lessons they have learned. Instead, both Adam and Eve become subject to tunnel-vision, getting so caught up in their own desires that they

132

fail to see the current situation in terms of divine order. Eve demonstrates her partial vision by suggesting that they divide their labors to increase their efficiency. Here she sees "work as a value in itself, cut off from the appointed order," which makes her ignore her proper priorities and put "efficiency before community."[60]

Adam responds initially with reason, putting everything into proper perspective: they are formed "not to irksome toile, but to delight" (IX: 242) and will soon have their children to help them in the garden. Thus he goes on for twenty lines, when he suddenly shifts to "But if much converse perhaps/ Thee satiate, to short absence I could yield" (247-28; italics mine). Why the abrupt change in Adam? Perhaps he sees Eve's look of disappointment at having her plan rejected and takes this rejection personally. At this point he, too, falls into partial vision, more desirous to please Eve and ensure her continued love than to consider the matter at hand rationally. His repetitive use of "But . . . But . . ." indicates his vacillation between his passion which produces partial vision, and reason, which reveals the whole picture to him. A few lines later, with "But other doubt possesses me," he returns to a rational frame of mind, recognizing the danger of Eve's working alone in the garden with the threat of Satan somewhere in their midst, and urges her not to leave his side.

Eve, however, taking this all too personally (again responding with partial vision) is insulted and hurt, feeling that Adam's hesitation in letting her go out alone means that he doesn't trust her. Now, what had originally been an effort to improve their gardening labors has become a chance to prove herself to Adam. Since Adam's doubts have made her feel inadequate, she wants to show off to win his respect and butter her own ego in the process. This predilection results in even more tunnel vision. Now Eve sees everything as a personal triumph or affront and forgets her duty to God within the greater framework of order.

Adam, again falling prey to Eve's beauty and his desire not to upset her, is unable to think clearly but grasps at any excuse to keep her from going. Impulsively, he tells her that temptation "asperses/ The tempted with dishonour foul" (296-97). Yet he should know better, for Raphael has just told him of Abdiel, whose heroic resistance to temptation has taught him otherwise. Even Eve is not convinced by Adam's rash statement. And, unfortunately, because she sees the flaws in this part of his argument and is preparing to answer it, her attention is drawn away when Adam finally hits upon the truth: "Suttle he needs must be, who could seduce/ Angels" (307-08). This warning goes right by Eve, for she concentrates instead on countering his first statement about the temptation, which, she maintains, "Sticks no dishonour on our Front, but turns/ Foul on himself" (330-31).

Then Eve turns to what many find a convincing argument: "And what is Faith, Love, Vertue unassaied"? (335), which echoes one of Milton's points in Areopagitica. However, there are several important distinctions between Milton's own argument and the one he puts into the mouth of Eve. Milton was writing his tract for a postlapsarian world, in which good and evil were everywhere--even within the mind of man--and to choose wisely one <u>must</u> be able to discern the difference. Uncensored reading was one important way to help him do just that. Eve, however, has no such need to learn about evil in her prelapsarian world. Furthermore, Milton was arguing for uncensored reading in order to prepare oneself for inevitable temptations but Eve was advocating a confrontation with the devil himself. She argues that "Faith, Love [and] Vertue" are worthless unless proven by trial, but she has forgotten that she has been tried each day by new experiences and that God has already ordained one principal trial for herself and Adam: obedience to his one command. That was the rightful way for her to prove herself, not to go out looking for trouble. Overcome by partial vision in her desire to impress Adam, Eve is unable to discern between courage and foolhardiness. Ironically, in attempting to "try" her virtue, she forgets to focus on serving God. Obviously seeking out temptation is really not the best way for Eve to fulfill her role in the divine plan either in relation to God or as Adam's wife but she does not realize this because at this point she cannot see beyond her own ego.

Adam, in a rational moment, warns Eve that the danger for them lies not in any kind of ambush in paradise, but within themselves, for "God left free the Will" to obey or disobey (351). Realizing that one may expect any manner of deceit from Satan, he cautions Eve to beware of misleading appearances:

> Least by some faire appeering good surpris'd
> She dictate false and misinforme the Will
> To do what God expressly hath forbid,"

(354-56)

--which is exactly what happens later as both of them are, in different ways, misled "by some faire appeering good." Eve chooses the appearance of good and Adam chooses an inferior good over obedience to God, the highest good.

In his final reply, Adam answers Eve's arguments with good reasons, responding to her protestations that he does not trust her by maintaining that with Satan loose in paradise she needs his protection. Furthermore, he tells her that they must both remind one another of the lessons and warnings they have received so as not to fall into temptation unawares:

> Not then mistrust, but tender love enjoynes,
> That I should mind thee oft, and mind thou me

since either one of them might well meet

> Some specious object by the Foe subornd,
> And fall into deception unaware.

(357-62)

134

--which, again, is exactly what happens, for Satan approaches Eve in the disguise of a serpent and catches her off guard and later Eve herself, "by the Foe subornd," surprises Adam with sin and temptation. Adam answers Eve's eagerness to prove herself with

> Seek not temptation then, which to avoide
> Were better . . .
> . . . Trial will come unsought.

(364-66)

And finally, if his reasons are not enough to convince her, he asserts his rightful authority in the divine order as her husband and protector:

> Wouldst thou approve thy constancie, approve
> First thy obedience.

(367-68)

Certainly, Adam is not convinced by Eve's argument, for he has just refuted it.[61] However, two lines later his entire tone changes:

> But if thou think, trial unsought may finde
> Us both securer then thus warnd thou seemst,
> Go; for thy stay, not free, absents thee more.

(370-73)

To what are we to attribute this abrupt change of mind? To what other than a look of hurt and resentment from Eve at his firmness, and her expression cuts Adam to the quick. Like an overly-permissive parent, he knows what is best for Eve but is afraid to enforce it at the risk of incurring her displeasure. In a moment of passion Adam dismisses both his knowledge and his reason. As Joseph Summers has explained, he "knows he is Eve's protector; but now he cares more for her immediate approval of him than he does for her immediate safety; he prefers the risk of her destruction to the risk of her momentary resentment."[62] Here Adam forgets the lesson he has learned from Raphael and surrenders to submissive weakness instead of affirming "self esteem, grounded on just and right." By failing to love and esteem himself and trust to his own better judgement, Adam has reverted to his petrarchan position, exalting Eve, degrading himself, and forgetting God. Furthermore, Adam's fear of offending Eve (when it is for her own good) is illogical, for how can he fear losing her when he is the only man on earth? Nevertheless, his fear of displeasing her or losing her love undermines his ability to affirm the courage of his convictions. Adam chooses a short range good over a long range good, forgetting what he had learned only the day before about the importance of seeing everything in perspective. His reason, if not totally extinguished at this point by his passionate impulse, would bring him to shame as he watches Eve toddle off like a naive child, saying confidently: "The willinger I go, nor much expect/ A Foe so proud will first the weaker seek"

135

(382-83). Eve has totally forgotten the story of the battle in heaven and expects Satan himself to play fair. And in this vulnerability Adam allows her to depart.

As Milton describes Eve, happily about her gardening tasks, he again underscores the point that leaving her by herself when an enemy had invaded Eden was a flagrant violation of right reason and right order. Eve ties up the flowers:

> Gently with Mirtle band, mindless the while,
> Her self, though fairest unsupported flour,
> From her best prop so farr, and storm so night.

(IX.431-33)

Eve appears more interested in caring for the flowers than in rightly taking care of herself, and Adam is more interested in pleasing Eve than in taking care of her. Both suffer from partial vision, which only gets worse as the temptation takes them further and further away from right order and finally brings them to the act of disobedience itself.

3. Temptation and the Fall: "The Mortal Sin Original"

Milton defines sin as disobedience, "the breaking of the law" and in Christian Doctrine he relates that Adam and Eve "broke every part of the law. . . . He was to be condemned both for trusting Satan and for not trusting God; he was faithless, ungrateful, disobedient, greedy, uxorious; she, negligent of her husband's welfare; both of them committed theft, robbery with violence, murder against their children (i.e. the whole human race); each was sacriligious and deceitful, cunningly aspiring to divinity although thoroughly unworthy of it, proud and arrogant" (p. 382). But let us turn from the many ramifications of their sin to an examination of its primary cause. Since the love of God, "which cherishes him above all other objects of glorification" (CD, p. 657), was for Milton the fulfillment of all law, the sins of both Adam and Eve are brought about by their inability to love correctly. First of all, both suffer from pride and a faulty sense of charity to themselves: Eve from "extravagant self-love" which makes her value herself above God (CD, p. 719); and Adam, as we have seen, from inadequate self-love and misplaced priorities.

In his temptation of Eve, Satan immediately inverts the order of love, addressing her in petrarchan terms, praising her above Adam, and saying that she should be worshipped by angels. Even Eve realizes that his "overpraising" is excessive (615); nevertheless, she listens to him and leaves her gardening to follow him to the tree, all her previous thoughts of efficiency now superceded. She knows that this one tree is forbidden to her and tells the serpent of God's prohibition. Yet Satan assaults her with reason, contradicting a truth which she had previously taken on faith with apparent logic and "occular proof." He has tasted and has not died-- a false statement, as we know, but even if it were true, what difference

136

should it make whatever a serpent does or does not eat? Adam and Eve are not to eat of the forbidden fruit: herein lies the measure of their obedience, their loyalty to God. Still, Satan continues to offer a barrage of "reasons" why she should ignore God's law and eat, resorting to logical double-talk like:

God therefore cannot hurt ye, and be just;
Not just, not God; not feard then, nor obeyd.

(700-01)

But still the law remains. Moreover, Eve should draw upon her recently-acquired knowledge of the war in heaven and the evidence of God's justice executed on the apostate angels to disprove this statement. However, leaving her no time for reflection or refutation, Satan builds the momentum and emotional appeal of his argument. The tree has been forbidden merely to keep her "low and ignorant" (704) when she and Adam could be "as gods" (708), he tells her, playing on her recently-developed desire to "prove herself," diabolically reversing the original situation. Like a high-pressure salesman who manipulates his customers into recognizing their need for his product, Satan assembles a myriad of reasons to convince Eve of her "need of this fair Fruit" (731). In addition, by now it is noon and Eve is hungry. Her five senses combine to second Satan's peroration: "to behold" (735) the fruit alone might tempt her, but added to that is "the sound" of Satan's words (736), and "the smell" of the fruit, which heightens her appetite (740), awakening in her a desire "to touch or taste" (742). Persuaded by satanic logic which inverts everything, turning good to evil, evil to good, she is led to see God's forbidding as all the more reason to eat the fruit, inferring "the good" (754) of it by its very prohibition: God has been keeping it all to himself, Satan argues.

Satan's rhetoric finally breaks down Eve's faith in God's law: "Such prohibitions binde not" she tells herself (760). Since God's law is apparently irrational, it thus ceases to exist. Eve's disobedience results from a breakdown of her faith.[63] Like Lucifer in his solipsistic argument about his creation, Eve has mistakenly made her reason alone the measure of all that is, even God's laws. As Milton realized, and Raphael had attempted to explain, there are some things one must take on faith. But ignoring her duty to love and obey her creator above all things, Eve brushes aside the importance of God's commandment, inverting the order of creation; totally misguided, she sees the fruit as "the Cure of all" (776).

As her disobedience is caused by a perversion of love and a denial of divine order, so her behavior after the Fall reflects this. Drunk with excitement, she observes no order of temperance in eating but gorges herself compulsively with the fruit. Then she begins to address the tree, promising to praise it in song every morning, an idolatrous parody of the morning hymns of praise she and Adam had offered to God. She bows to it as she leaves: an obvious inversion of divine order when a human being worships a plant. Her relationship with God, now void of love, turns to fear. She sees her Father and creator as "Our great Forbidder, safe with all his Spies" and like any disobedient child, she only hopes that he has not seen her (815).

Her thoughts of Adam also reveal an inversion in love and order. Perhaps, she muses, she will keep this knowledge to herself:

> And render me more equal, and perhaps,
> A thing not undesirable, somtime
> Superior; for inferior who is free?

> (823-25)

Echoing satanic logic she inverts the entire marriage order. But the threat of death and the possibility of "<u>Adam</u> wedded to another <u>Eve</u>" (826) convince her to share with Adam "in bliss or woe:/ So dear I love him" (831-32). Obviously, this is also a prideful inversion of love in that she is thinking of what is best for herself, not Adam. C.S. Lewis has even called Eve a murderess for sharing the apple with Adam, although A.J.A. Waldock has spoken up in her defence, arguing that she did not really know what death was.[64] Her decision at this point reflects, at best, jealousy and possessive love, <u>cupiditas</u>, not the <u>caritas</u> of love within divine order.

After deciding what to tell Adam, Eve appears, full of excuses and dissimulation. The couple's nakedness in the State of Innocence had been not only physical but psychological, for they had had nothing to hide from each other. But now the fallen Eve covers her offense with flattery and lies: "Thee I have misst, and thought it long, depriv'd/ Thy presence, agonie of love till now/ Not felt" (857-59) when actually she has been too busy with the serpent to miss Adam at all. Adam and Eve are no longer "naked"--open--in their relationship with one another but will from now on have to cope with the dissimulation and facades that fallen people put between them, concealing their true selves behind words and actions just as Adam and Eve will later hide their bodies with fig leaves.

"O fairest of Creation, last and best/ Of all God's works"--Adam's first words reveal the lapse into petrarchanism that will dominate his reaction (896-96). In his love and concern for Eve, he has inverted the natural order, forgetting that he--because of his greater intellect--is the "best" of God's creations on earth. Basing his response on the false premise of her superiority, undervaluing himself and God's order, he sets up a chain of reasoning which limits his reaction to the inevitable:

> with thee
> Certain my resolution is to Die;
> How can I live without thee?

> (906-08)

Adam chooses to die, suffering from what Milton described in <u>Christian Doctrine</u> as a "perverse hatred of" himself, a category which includes

138

suicides and "those who sin wilfully and deliberately" (p. 719). Both of these pertain to Adam, who knowingly and wilfully disobeys God's commandment and eats the fruit, choosing to die rather than to live without Eve, whom he prizes more than his own worth, more than God, and loves more than life itself.

Many critics have seen Adam's decision as inherently noble. Northrop Frye maintains that it "impresses us, in our fallen state, as a heroic decision."[65] Such is the romantic matter of operas like Verdi's Aida and Wagner's Tristan and Isolde and love tragedies like Shakespeare's Romeo and Juliet. A.J.A. Waldock has seen Adam's fall as a result of "love as human beings know it at its best."[66] Yet as compelling and dramatic as this Liebestod seems, is it really all that commendable, or even necessary in Adam's case?

H.V.S. Ogden calls Adam's predicament "tragic" because he must choose "between obedience to God and love of Eve."[67] However, we would do well to consider who promulgates this tragic predicament: certainly not God. Rather, Adam himself allows his love of Eve to dominate his consciousness, making him forget the whole picture. His partial vision fragments and then polarizes what had been designed as an all-encompassing hierarchy of love. He was to love God and to love Eve and the rest of creation, but suddenly he has opposed love of the creature to that of the creator. Blinded by her beauty and his fear of losing her, he fails to see any viable alternatives wherein he might still love both God and Eve (interceding for her, perhaps). He gives up in despair of having both and chooses the lesser, more immediate good. Adam's sin is a failure to love wisely within the divine order: "If conjugal love were the highest value in Adam's world, then of course his resolve would have been the correct one."[68] But he has, in Aristotelian terms, chosen a lesser good in preference to the supreme good,[69] like many tragic heroes loving "not wisely, but too well." And for this error Eve embraces him:

> much won that he his Love
> Had so enobl'd, as of choice to incurr
> Divine displeasure for her sake, or Death.

(991-93)

Thomas Traherne, like Milton, realized that human life involves not merely a series of simple choices between good and evil but that we, like Adam, are often faced with moral dilemmas, forced to choose between two different goods. Traherne recognized that "Things Good in themselves, when they stand in Competition with those that are better, have the notion of Evil: Better Things are Evil, if compared with the Best; especially where the Choice of the one hinders the Acquisition of the other" (CE, p. 15). Like Milton, he stressed the importance of priorities, the importance of seeing everything in perspective, and warned of the dangers of partial vision. Loving, which Traherne saw as a basic human tendency, could bring men to ruin if they did not learn to love "the World aright." Some of his discussion in Christian Ethicks could almost be used as a

139

commentary upon Adam's fall in <u>Paradise Lost</u>. Traherne warned that "If by our voluntary Remisness, or Mistake, or Disorder, we dote upon one Object, or suffer some few things to engage our Souls so intirely, as to forget and neglect all the rest, we rob all those we desert, of their due Esteem, and abridge our selves of that Liberty and Extent, wherein the greatness of our soul consisteth" (p. 53). Adam, by doting upon Eve's beauty, forgets to see her in perspective, thus robbing himself, God, and Eve herself of "due Esteem" within the divine plan. In so doing, Adam has most obviously abridged his own liberty, enslaving himself and his posterity to sin and death.

By disobeying God for the love of Eve, Adam cuts himself off from God, who is the source of all love. As Arnold Stein points out, "Adam can neither love himself adequately nor love Eve as himself unless he can love God adequately--and so make his love for Eve, the unity of their shared self, an expression of that higher love."[70] By choosing to love Eve instead of God, Adam consequently makes her his god, but this idolatry is motivated by his own desires, not by a consideration of what is in her best interests.[71] Thus, ironically enough, by choosing to worship her and removing her from her proper place in the divine order, he has begun to relate to her as an object--a gilded object, perhaps, but still an object. He has enshrined her beauty but forgotten to see her as a person, ignoring what was really best for Eve.

Carrying this argument a bit further, Helen Gardner claims that what appears as a noble, unselfish act is actually a product of Adam's selfishness: "It is for his own sake, to escape the horror of solitude, for the sake of love rather than for her sake, he decides to share her fate."[72] Indeed, nowhere does Adam attempt to share her punishment, to make it lighter. Rather, he cries out in romantic despair: "we are one/ One Flesh; to lose thee were to loose my self" (958-59; italics mine). Ultimately then, Adam is a petrarchan lover, more concerned with his own suffering than with Eve's fate; he feels that life without Eve is simply not worth living, so he chooses to die. Furthermore, as we recall from the accounts in Burton's <u>Anatomy</u> and other discussions of suicide throughout the period, suicide was symptomatic of the sin of despair, which was caused by a lack of faith. Adam, as we have seen, submits "to what seemd remediless" (919), in his concern with the momentous matter at hand forgetting, hence denying, the power of God. Nowhere does he pray for aid, for guidance, or even acknowledge that it is within God's power to help him. He, like Eve, sins from an excessive concentration on the self, a distorted definition of love, and a manifest lack of faith. Neither of them learned the lesson that Raphael had tried so hard to teach them.

4. The State of Misery: Division and Disorder

By separating themselves from divine order by their disobedience, Adam and Eve bring the disorder of the State of Misery into their once-perfect world. Their sin has both immediate and far-reaching effects. An early example is the disorder of their fallen appetites. Like Eve, who

had devoured the fruit with a compulsive appetite heretofore unknown in
Eden, Adam, intoxicated by his sin, now leers at Eve with a new gleam in
his eye:

> Eve, now I see thou art exact of taste
> . . .
> Much pleasure we have lost, . . .
> . . . nor known till now
> True relish, tasting; if such pleasure be
> In things to us forbidden, it might be wish'd,
> For this one Tree had bin forbidden ten.
> But come, so well refresh't, now let us play,
> As meet is, after such delicious Fare;
> For never did thy Beautie since the day
> I saw thee first and wedded thee, adorn'd
> With all perfections, so enflame my sense
> With ardor to enjoy thee.

(IX.1017, 1022-31; italics mine)

His adoration of Eve now reduced to carnal appetite, he sees her as merely an object to "enjoy," to satisfy his hunger. Love removed from divine
order degenerates into lust and caritas is reduced to cupiditas.[73]

   Adam and Eve awaken from their "grosser sleep" (1049) in a state
of mental and physical disorder, their intoxication with sin leading inevi-
tably to a virtual hangover of misery and guilt. Their State of Innocence
gone, they are "naked left/ To guiltie shame" (1057-58). Having cut themselves off from the sustaining grace of God and unity with all creation,
they are now overwhelmed by a sense of inadequacy and alienation. Adam
wonders how he will ever face God or the angels again and hides himself
in the darkness of the forest. Northrop Frye sees their shame as "something deeper and more sinister . . . than simply the instinctive desire to
cover the genital organs. It is . . . the emotional response to the sin of
pride."[74] Now they experience the very reverse of the exultation they
had felt earlier, when they had wilfully exalted themselves and negated
their union with God. In the State of Misery they realize the bitter consequence of this negation, the inadequacy of the self without God. They
seek to cover their embarrassment with fig leaves but, stripped of their
faith, their love, their self-respect, they are far more naked inside.

   As Roland Frye has so well expressed it, they are alienated "from
God, from themselves, and from each other."[75] Whereas in the State of
Innocence the love of God and one another had ordered their lives, now
in Misery they are afflicted with disorder on all levels. Stripped of their
peace of mind, they are alienated from themselves:

> high Passions, Anger, Hate,
> Mistrust, Suspicion, Discord . . . shook sore
> Their inward State of Mind"

(1123-25)

Their inversion of the natural order has had its stormy repercussions within them, as their passions have overruled their reason:

> For Understanding rul'd not, and the Will
> Heard not her lore, both in subjection now
> To sensual Appetite.

(1127-29)

Nor are they able to comfort one another in their distress, for their inner discord only comes between them in the first argument in paradise. Their loss of love for one another is the inevitable result of cutting themselves off from God, the source of all love. Sinning out of excessive self-love, like Satan, they have become isolated in themselves, unable to find relief in communication. Instead, they either soliloquize, wallowing in despair and self-pity, or spend their time in mutual accusation, Adam blaming Eve for going off by herself and Eve reproaching him for his lack of firmness in allowing her to do so. Thus they come skulking out at the summons of their creator:

> Love was not in thir looks, either to God
> Or to each other, but apparent guilt,
> And shame, and perturbation, and despaire,
> Anger, and obstinacie, and hate, and guile.

(X.111-14)

The discord they embody extends even to the rest of their world, as the once mild weather becomes a disordered series of storms and extremes of heat and cold. And perhaps even sadder, their denial of love and order extends even to the animals that had once played together and been their friends. Discord afflicts them too; they begin to devour each other and flee from human beings as the order of love turns to enmity throughout all creation. Such were the many aspects of the State of Misery, the "death" which came upon the world as a result of original sin. As Milton explained in Christian Doctrine, "every evil, and everything which seems to lead to destruction, is indeed under the name of death" (p. 393). It was not physical death alone that Adam and Eve brought upon themselves and their progeny, but a world of diseases and disorders, all resulting from a denial of their harmony with God.

5. The State of Grace

"Man's restoration," Milton wrote in Christian Doctrine, "is the act by which man, freed from sin and death by God the Father through Jesus Christ, is raised to a far more excellent state of grace and glory than that from which he fell" (p. 415). As sin and the State of Misery arose from defective love and disobedience, salvation in the State of Grace would be accomplished by the Son's compassionate love and perfect obedience, willingly sacrificing himself with humility to offset Adam's and

142

Eve's willful egotism and pride. Thus, Milton explained, "Heav'nly love shall outdoo Hellish hate" (III.298), foiling all of Satan's plans and overcoming evil with good. For Milton, as we shall see, the Son provides not only the means of salvation for Adam and Eve but also a model of "the better fortitude" of unselfish love and obedience, which all mankind must follow in their regeneration.

In Book III, God explains his plans to redeem mankind:

> once more I will renew
> [their] lapsed powers, though forfeit and enthrall'd
> By sin to foul exorbitant desires.

> (175-77)

Furthermore, he announces:

> Some I have chosen of peculiar grace
> Elect above the rest; so is my will (183-84)

As Milton demonstrates here and describes at length in Christian Doctrine, he believed that Christ's redemption offered the State of Grace "to all sinners, not only to the elect "but that some were given peculiar grace as examples to the rest (p. 448). Thus, in Paradise Lost he portrays God announcing his plan of grace for mankind:

> The rest shall hear me call, and oft be warnd
> Thir sinful state, and to appease betimes
> Th'incensed Deitie, while offerd grace
> Invites; for I will cleer thir senses dark,
> What may suffice, and soften stonie hearts
> To pray, repent, and bring obedience due"

> (185-90)

Yet the Redemption required a combination of God's grace and human faith. As they had sinned through a lack of faith, now Adam and Eve must answer God's call by manifesting his faith in order to be redeemed. Grace, as Milton described it in Christian Doctrine, involved a calling or "vocation" from God--"the rest shall hear me call"--and a renewal of our lapsed powers, "whereby the mind and will of the natural man are partially renewed and are divinely moved towards knowledge of God" (p. 457) so that we might be strengthened and given a chance to respond with faith and repent. Such is the prevenient grace which the Son brings to Adam and Eve in Paradise Lost when he clothes their "inward nakedness" with his "Robe of righteousness" (X.221-22) and which enables them to repent, removing "The stonie from their hearts," making "new flesh/ Regenerate grow instead" (XI.4-5).

Regeneration, according to Milton, falls into the degrees of "recognition of sin, contrition, confession, abandonement of evil and conversion to good," all of which we can see taking place in Adam and Eve in Book X. Milton also adds concerning confession that "sometimes sins are confessed to God. . . . sometimes to men" (CD, p. 468). As we shall see, Adam and Eve will do both. For much of Book X, Adam is overcome by despair, crying out for death to come and take him, until Eve makes the first effort at reconciliation, offering "soft words to his passion" (865), her concern for him a gesture of caritas. As he bitterly reproves her, she throws herself in tears at his feet (contrition) and seeks his pardon, confessing that she is:

> More miserable; both have sind, but thou
> Against God onely, I against God and thee.

> (930-31)

Admitting her sin to herself (recognition) and to him (confession), she repents for having offended and will, she says, "importune Heaven" that she may bear the blame for both (933). Eve's unselfish desire to bear the blame for Adam represents a reversal of her earlier selfish desire to share the apple with him and damn him with herself.[76]

Adam, at this point, while correcting Eve for her impulsive offer, relents and also exhibits recognition, contrition, and confession. He regrets his sin and says if it were possible he would ask

> That on my head all might be visited,
> Thy frailtie and infirmer Sex forgiv'n,
> To me committed and by me expos'd.

> (955-57)

Adam has previously shown his contrition for his sin, but now confesses to Eve that he has neglected his responsibility to her.

The next steps in regeneration are abandonment of evil and conversion to good. In reaching out in unselfish love for one another, Adam and Eve have abandoned the selfish love that had led them to sin. And as Adam again asserts his proper role in the order of marriage, we see them turning to an active affirmation of love (conversion to good) between them. They will no longer blame each other

> but strive
> In offices of Love, how we may light'n
> Each others burden in our share of woe.

> (959-61)

Resuming his role as her husband and protector, Adam comforts Eve in her despair, rejecting her suggestions that they kill themselves or remain barren so as not to transmit sin and misery to their offspring, consoling her with the thought that her seed will bruise the serpent's head. Adam counsels that they <u>bear</u> their penance, not wilfully seek to escape it:

> No more be mention'd then of violence
> Against our selves, and wilful barrenness,
> That cuts us off from hope, and savours onely
> Rancor and pride, impatience and despite,
> Reluctance against God and his just yoke
> Laid on our Necks

(1041-46)

Here their conversion to good extends to their relationship with God and represents the beginnings of the Christian heroism of patience and obedience to God's law, not "reluctance against God and his just yoke." As Milton wrote of his own lesson in patience in sonnet XIX: "Who best/ Bear his mild yoke, they serve him best."[77] Accepting with patience his burden of penance, Adam has reinstated himself as a willing servant of God.

With this resolution Adam and Eve return to the place of their judgement and confess their sins to God, formally re-establishing their relationship with their creator. This confession includes all of the previously-mentioned degrees of penance. Their recognition of sin and their confessions are exhibited as they admit their faults and humbly beg pardon; their contrition is shown in their tears and sighs "sent from hearts contrite" (X. 1103); and their humble return to ask their creator's pardon represents their decision to abandon evil and convert to good. Their initial efforts at reconciliation with God lead them to a sense of spiritual renewal as their prayers are answered with God's grace, bringing them

> Strength added from above, new hope to spring
> Out of despaire, joy, but with fear yet linkt.

(XI.138-39)

6. The Final Books: Adam's Lesson in Christian Heroism

As Adam and Eve leave Eden, they receive further instructions which will help them cope with this postlapsarian world. When Michael reveals to Adam the panorama of future history, he gives him a lesson in Christian heroism, the way of

> True patience, and to temper joy with fear
> And pious sorrow, equally enur'd
> By moderation either state to beare;
> Prosperous or adverse.

(XI.361-64)

Although some critics have complained that the last books are unrelated to the rest of the poem, thematically they are essential. In terms of the

145

the Four Estates, Adam and Eve need the lessons they learn in the final two books to complete their regeneration in the State of Grace and learn of the promised State of Glory. The "very joy" they experience at the beginning of Book XI is, according to Lawrence Sasek, "a sign of instability, while Eve's pleasure in the physical environment shows excessive regard for the material, a degree of spiritual blindness."[78] Michael gives Adam and Eve a more complete understanding of their sin and teaches them how to live a virtuous life in this our fallen world. As Thomas Traherne also emphasized throughout <u>Christian Ethicks</u>, Adam and Eve before the Fall had lived by a much simpler code of ethics, but fallen men and women must learn to develop virtues which were unknown to Adam and Eve in the State of Innocence. Thus, as Adam and Eve are forced to leave the garden, in <u>Paradise Lost</u> they are given another lesson in a continuous process of education, receiving from Michael the truths which will help them face the trials of the postlapsarian world. Without the knowledge of the redemption, Adam and Eve's regeneration would be theologically incomplete and they would be left hanging somewhere between the State of Misery and the promised State of Grace. Finally, it seems that Milton wanted Adam to be "one of us," that we might evolve with him during the course of the poem from the Old Adam to the New, learning our biblical history and the personal lessons it holds for us. Thus, he brings Adam into our world at the end of the poem, that we might begin where he left off, accepting the lessons of love and service that make our current State of Misery into a State of Grace. Milton's readers, as well as Adam, are told of the virtues of patience and temperance that they will need in this postlapsarian world.

Furthermore, Adam and Eve must be taught the lessons of the last two books in order to complete the process of regeneration outlined in Milton's <u>Christian Doctrine</u>. As we have seen, the first phase of their regeneration had consisted of prevenient grace: calling and partial renewal of their lapsed powers, which enabled them to repent. But for Milton, their conversion to grace also required a second, more complete process of repentence and regeneration which involved an awareness of the redemption and the consequences of their sin. Milton believed that the first phase of repentance produced contrition for one's sins primarily because of the punishment involved. Adam and Eve's punishment had been immediate: their suffering in the State of Misery; for their posterity, this first level of contrition would also be motivated by fear of damnation. However, in the more perfect contrition of regeneration, according to Milton, one repents because his sins have offended God (<u>CD</u>, p. 466).

In order to bring Adam to this level of repentance, Michael must first show him the enormous magnitude of his sin, by revealing its consequences: death in all its various forms--murder, sickness, and a world of misery. Realizing what misery he has brought to the world, Adam bursts into tears, although it would seem his immediate sorrow is more for his hapless progeny than for having offended God. Nevertheless, a realization of the extent of the sin and misery he has brought to the world, juxtaposed with God's mercy in the redemption, ultimately increases the love and gratitude Adam feels for his creator. "Saving faith," the second part of the regenerative process, requires a knowledge of the redemption, for so "we believe, on the authority of God's promise, that all those things which God has promised us in Christ are ours, and especially the grace of eternal life" (CD, p. 248). Adam and Eve leave paradise with "saving grace" because Michael has revealed to them God's promise of Grace and Glory. As Mary Ann Radzinowicz maintains, "Adam goes down into the world as a Christian, in his lifetime having been vouchsafed a foreknowledge of the redeemer."[79]

Adam has been given this foreknowledge of the redeemer as a means of Salvation not only in a general but in a specific sense. Christ and all the "types of Christ" who anticipate him by demonstrating love and obedience unite to form a model of conduct for Adam and all aspiring Christians. The final books of Paradise Lost pick up the theme of the hero and anti-hero Milton had developed in Books I, II, IV, V, and VI, playing satanic types who embody pride and disobedience against types of Christ who represent their antithesis. One satanic type in Book XII is Nimrod, a man

> Of proud ambitious heart, who was not content
> With fair equalitie, fraternal state,
> Will arrogate Dominion undeserv'd
> Over his brethren.

> (25-28)

Nimrod's pride and selfish ambition echo Satan's and contrast with "the better fortitude" of Enoch, Noah, Abraham, and the others, and, of course, that of Christ. Milton has Michael employ the method of comparison/contrast to teach Adam and his progeny to differentiate between false heroism and true, as the last two books become a panorama of obedience and disobedience, good and evil. The lesson, repeated again and again throughout Paradise Lost for Adam's benefit and our own is essentially that of Luke 14:11: "Whosoever exalteth himself shall be abased; and he that humbleth himself shall be exalted." Satan, choosing the way of pride, has exalted himself to be abased, and, as Adam will shortly see, the Messiah will, in humbling himself, be exalted. This is the way of true heroism, but as Milton realized, the world, grounded in physical appearances, is given to admiring the flamboyant gesture, the "glory" of worldly conquest. As Michael tells Adam, this fallen world is too easily inclined to admire the mere appearance of virtue:

> For in those dayes Might onely shall be admir'd,
> And Valour and Heroic Vertue call'd;
> To overcome in Battle, and subdue
> Nations, and bring home spoils with infinite
> Man-slaughter, shall be held the highest pitch
> Of human Glorie . . . .
> Thus Fame shall be atchiev'd, renown on Earth,
> And what most merits fame in silence hid.

> (XI.689-99)

147

And even with his angelic tutor beside him, Adam himself later falls into the same human error of equating "might" with heroism. As Michael tells him of the Messiah, Adam rejoices, expecting to see the serpent get his head bruised in a glorious fight. But Michael patiently corrects him: "Dream not of their fight/ As of a duel" (XII.386-87). The Messiah, he tells Adam, will overcome evil not in some swashbuckling physical combat, but in an exercise of spiritual strength:

> by fulfilling that which thou didst want,
> Obedience to the Law of God, impos'd
> On penaltie of death, and suffering death,
> The penaltie to thy transgression due.

(396-99)

Undeniably less "exciting" than the superficial heroics admired by fallen mankind, this true heroism, Michael explains, is infinitely more admirable, winning fame in the eyes of God and the reward of eternal life. The angel continues his lesson, emphasizing that:

> So onely can high Justice rest appaid.
> The Law of God exact he shall fulfill
> Both by obedience and by love, though love
> Alone fulfill the Law

(401-04; italics mine)

Thus, as Milton shows us, Christ will fulfill the law, broken by disobedience and love, an example for all mankind. Adam learns to admire and emulate what is for Milton the true form of heroism. With greater wisdom and humility he repeats his lesson to Michael:

> Henceforth I learne that to obey is best,
> And love with fear the onely God, to walk
> As in his presence, ever to observe
> His providence, and on him sole depend,
> Mercifull over all his works, with good
> Still overcoming evil, and by small
> Accomplishing great things.

(XII.561-67)

Adam's lesson and ultimately the lesson of Paradise Lost is man's proper role in this world, as he sees his life within the pattern of the Four Estates. This awareness is the "paradise within" with which Adam and Eve leave what had once been the State of Innocence and journey into our world of greater trials but also greater blessings. Following the example set for them by the Son, Milton's readers were, like Adam and Eve, expected to follow the way of humility, recognizing themselves as children of God, and responding with the "true filial freedom" of obedience and love. This is the Christian heroism that Milton affirmed throughout his works, a heroism which leads individuals into the State of Grace and not, like its epic counterpart, into pride and the State of Misery. In seeking to redefine heroism in a Christian context, Milton resembles his contemporary Thomas Traherne, who explained in Christian Ethicks that "Divine Vertues (which we put instead of the Heathenish Heroical,) are such as have only GOD for their Object and End, but their Pattern and Example. They are Vertues which are seen in his eternal Life, by Practicing which are changed into the same Image, and are made partakers of the Divine Nature" (p. 24). Such a model Milton endorsed in Paradise Lost, showing us in the fall of Satan that following the way of pride and seeking to be more than this, invariably makes one less. This fundamental message which Milton held out to his readers echoes the sentiments of George Herbert, who wrote:

> These are thy wonders, Lord of love,
> To make us see we are but flowers that glide:
>   Which when we once can finde and prove,
> Thou hast a garden for us, where to bide.
>   Who would be more,
>   Swelling through store,
> Forfeit their Paradise by their pride.[80]

("The Flower," ll. 43-49)

Thus, like Herbert, Traherne, and many others among his contemporaries, Milton sought to teach his readers to "find and prove" their spiritual identity. For this reason he led them in Paradise Lost through a maze of sin and temptation so that they might see and know and thus avoid such temptations in their own lives, abjuring the way of pride which was responsible for their Misery and affirming instead the heroism of the "true wayfaring Christian,"[81] seeking the States of Grace and Glory.

NOTES

[1]Thomas Traherne, Centuries of Meditations in Centuries, Poems, and Thanksgivings, ed. H.M. Margoliouth (Oxford: Clarendon Press, 1958), I, 4. All references to the Centuries are from this edition and will hereafter be cited and abbreviated (as C) in the text.

[2]Paradise Lost in The Works of John Milton, ed. Frank Allen Patterson et al. (New York: Columbia Univ. Press, 1931), II. All quotations from Paradise Lost are from this edition and will hereafter be noted in the text.

[3]Frank Kermode, "Adam Unparadised," in Paradise Lost: An Authoritative Text, Backgrounds and Sources, Criticism, ed. Scott Elledge (New York: Norton, 1975), p. 491.

[4]Stanley E. Fish, Surprised by Sin: The Reader in Paradise Lost (Berkeley: Univ. of California Press, 1971), p. 1 and passim.

[5]Thomas Traherne, <u>Christian Ethicks</u>, ed. Carol L. Marks and George Robert Guffey (Ithaca: Cornell Univ. Press, 1968), pp. 118, 146. All references to <u>Christian Ethicks</u> are from this edition and will hereafter be cited (and abbreviated <u>CE</u>) in the text.

[6]This confusion, according to Traherne, was strongly reinforced by the notion of private property, which makes people perceive themselves and one another in terms as limited as their material goods, disregarding entirely their spiritual inheritance. In his frequent tirades against private property Traherne seems to approach the beliefs of Gerrard Winstanley, founder of the Diggers, who also believed that "Adam's innocency is the time of child-hood" and that private property served to perpetuate the State of Misery: "I demand, whether all wars, blood-shed, and misery came not upon the Creation, when one man endeavoured to be Lord over another, and to claim propriety in the earth above another? Your Scripture will prove this sufficiently to be true. And whether this Misery shall not remove (and not till then) when all the branches of mankind shall look upon themselves as one man, and upon the earth as a common Treasury to all." <u>The New Law of Righteousness</u> (1649) in <u>The Works of Gerrard Winstanley</u>, ed. George H. Sabine (Ithaca, N.Y.; Cornell Univ. Press, 1941), p. 212 and <u>A Letter to the Lord Fairfax</u>, <u>Works</u>, p. 290.

[7]Northrop Frye, <u>The Return of Eden: Five Essays on Milton's Epics</u> (Toronto: Univ. of Toronto Press, 1965), p. 33. Some confusion has arisen concerning Milton's use of the term, "begotten," for surely if the Son had participated in the creation of the angels, he must have existed prior to this official announcement. But as Milton explained in <u>Christian Doctrine</u>, the Son had simply not yet been magnified and announced as such. For a discussion of this, see <u>The Englishman John Milton's Two Books of Investigation into Christian Doctrine Drawn from the Sacred Scripture Alone</u>, trans. John Carey in <u>Complete Prose Works of John Milton</u>, ed. Don M. Wolfe et al. (New Haven: Yale Univ. Press, 1973), VI, 205-06. All references to <u>Christian Doctrine</u> are from this edition which will hereafter be abbreviated <u>CD</u> and documented in my text.

[8]Harold Toliver, "The Splinter Coalition," in <u>New Essays on Paradise Lost</u>, ed. Thomas Kranidas (Berkeley: Univ. of California Press, 1971), p. 44.

[9]<u>The City of God</u>, XIV, xiii, in <u>Basic Writings of St. Augustine</u>, ed. Whitney J. Oates (New York: Random House, 1948), II, 257-58.

[10]Arnold Stein, <u>Answerable Style: Essays on Paradise Lost</u> (Minneapolis: Univ. of Minnesota Press, 1953), p. 75.

[11]<u>John Milton: Complete Poems and Major Prose</u>, ed. Merritt Y. Hughes (New York: Odyssey Press, 1957), p. 733. All references to <u>Areopagitica</u> are from this text.

[12]Fish, p. 332.

[13]Jackson Cope, The Metaphoric Structure of Paradise Lost (Baltimore: Johns Hopkins Univ. Press, 1962), p. 82.

[14]Helen Gardner, A Reading of Paradise Lost (Oxford: Clarendon Press, 1965), p. 59.

[15]Fish, p. 162.

[16]James Holly Hanford, A Milton Handbook, 3rd. ed. (New York: F.S. Crofts, 1939), p. 177.

[17]Ibid., p. 60.

[18]Stein, pp. 20ff.

[19]Fish, p. 49.

[20]Gardner, p. 31.

[21]Some Graver Subject: An Essay on Paradise Lost (New York: Schocken, 1967), pp. 73-74.

[22]Areopagitica, Hughes, p. 728.

[23]Louis Martz, The Paradise Within: Studies in Vaughan, Traherne, and Milton (New Haven: Yale Univ. Press, 1964), p. 124.

[24]An interesting point here, for Milton, usually the champion of free will, seems to lean strongly in the direction of determinism.

[25]Stein, p. 23; see also Broadbent, pp. 219-220.

[26]Many critics, among them Harold Toliver (p. 40), and Helen Gardner (pp. 67-68), have seen the war in heaven as Milton's metaphor for all poltiical turmoil. It is, according to Gardner, "an epitome of the wars of history," beginning with "pride, pomp and circumstance and images of heroism [and ending] with horrible indignity and senseless destruction."

[27]The Holy Bible, Conteyning the Old Testament, and the New: Newly Translated out of the Originall Tongues, & with the former Translations diligently compared and revised by his Majesties speciall Commandement. Appointed to be read in Churches (London, 1611). All biblical quotations are taken from this text.

[28]"Lycidas," l. 78, in Hughes, p. 122.

[29]Of course, as C.S. Lewis has explained in A Preface to Paradise Lost (London: Oxford Univ. Press, 1942), p. 95, the very fact that Satan could not remember his beginnings "proves that those beginnings lay outside" himself.

[30] Several contemporary studies, among them Godfrey Goodman's The Fall of Man and Robert Burton's Anatomy of Melancholy equated disease with sin, seeing disease as an indication that one was in the State of Misery. In fact, Burton recommended prayer and spiritual counseling as well as a special diet as a cure for various digestive disturbances. Melancholy was for him both a spiritual and a physical disorder and its ultimate cure was redemption to the State of Grace, the attainment of spiritual health originally lost in the Fall.

[31] That is, if one is motivated like Satan by pride instead of altruistic love.

[32] Fish, pp. 18-19.

[33] Gardner, p. 62.

[34] C.A. Patrides, Milton and the Christian Tradition (Oxford: Clarendon Press, 1966), p. 171.

[35] Kermode, p. 500.

[36] Broadbent, p. 36.

[37] Sister Mary Irma Corcoran, Milton's Paradise with Reference to the Hexameral Background (Washington, D.C.; Catholic Univ. of America Press, 1945; rpt. 1967), p. 17.

[38] B. Rajan, Paradise Lost and the Seventeenth-Century Reader (London: Chatto and Windus, 1947), p. 56.

[39] Hanford, pp. 203, 235.

[40] Hughes, p. 733.

[41] A.J.A. Waldock, Paradise Lost and Its Critics (Cambridge: Cambridge Univ. Press, 1947; rpt. 1961), p. 125.

[42] E.M.W. Tillyard, Milton (London: Chatto and Windus, 1930), pp. 282-83.

[43] Broadbent, p. 177.

[44] Barbara Kiefer Lewalski, "Innocence and Experience in Milton's Eden," in New Essays on Paradise Lost, ed. Thomas Kranidas (Berkeley: Univ. of California Press, 1971), pp. 86-117.

[45] Lewalski, p. 93.

[46] Fish, p. 226. See also J.M. Evans, Paradise Lost and the Genesis Tradition (Oxford: Clarendon Press, 1968), p. 246 and Arthur E. Barker,

"Paradise Lost" The Relevance of Regeneration," in Paradise Lost: A Tercentenary Tribute, ed. Balachandra Rajan (Toronto: Univ. of Toronto Press, 1967), p. 60.

[47]City of God, XIV, x, p. 254. See also Patrides, p. 108ff.

[48]Sir Thomas Browne, Religio Medici, ed. F.L. Huntley (New York: Appleton Century Crofts, 1966), pp. 49-50.

[49]The Eloquent 'I': Style and Self in Seventeenth-Century Prose (Madison: Univ. of Wisconsin Press, 1968), p. 7.

[50]Milton's Conception of Sin as Developed in Paradise Lost, Utah State University Monograph Series, Vol. VII, No. 5 (Logan Utah: Utah State Univ. Press, 1960), p. 60.

[51]Patrides, p. 105.

[52]See Lewalski's discussion of this experience, pp. 100-01.

[53]Northrop Frye (p. 75) sees her dream as "Freudian wish-fulfillment," and C.A. Patrides (p. 106) agrees, calling it "a projection of her innermost desires and aspirations"; H.V.S. Ogden argues that it "infects her will" in "The Crisis of Paradise Lost Reconsidered," in Milton: Modern Essays in Criticism, ed. Arthur E. Barker (New York: Oxford Univ. Press, 1965), p. 320; and Arnold Stein (P. 93) sees it as "a wedge for separating Eve from Adam by returning her to her mirror-state."

[54]Patrick, p. 30.

[55]Lewalski, p. 103.

[56]Fish, pp. 22-23.

[57]The Enclosed Garden: Tradition and the Image in Seventeenth-Century Poetry (Madison: Univ. of Wisconsin Press, 1966), pp. 31-45 passim.

[58]Broadbent, p. 246.

[59]Waldock, p. 109.

[60]Stein, p. 94 and Broadbent, p. 255. See also Joseph H. Summers, The Muse's Method: An Introduction to Paradise Lost (New York: Norton, 1962), p. 170; Broadbent, p. 255. Regardless of Milton's Puritan background, one must conclude that he meant her attitude here to be regarded as wrong in paradise.

[61]Citing the power of Eve's argument, Dennis Burden, in The Logical Epic: A Study of the Argument in Paradise Lost (Cambridge, Mass.: Harvard Univ. Press, 1967), p. 89, claims that Adam is overcome by her logic

and not by his passion. However, a close examination of the text at this point will demonstrate that although many readers may be convinced by her argument (perhaps merely another way for Milton to "bait" his readers and surprise them with a demonstration of their sinful natures in the manner suggested by Stanley Fish), Adam, most certainly, is not.

[62]Summers, p. 174.

[63]Cf. John S. Diekhoff, Milton's Paradise Lost: A Commentary on the Argument (New York: Humanities Press, 1958), p. 133 and Fish, p. 245.

[64]Lewis, p. 121; Waldock, p. 63.

[65]Frye, p. 79.

[66]Waldock, p. 52.

[67]Ogden, p. 321.

[68]Lewis, p. 123.

[69]See John M. Steadman, Milton's Epic Characters: Image and Idol (Chapel Hill: Univ. of North Carolina Press, 1968), p. 32ff. for a discussion of Milton's use of Aristotelian principles.

[70]Stein, p. 115.

[71]Roland Mushat Frye, God, Man and Satan: Patterns of Christian Thought and Life in Paradise Lost, Pilgrim's Progress, and the Great Theologians (Port Washington, N.Y.: Kennikat Press, 1972), pp. 54-55; Fish, pp. 335-36.

[72]Gardner, p. 90.

[73]As Summers explains (p. 106), each of the lovers becomes for the other "merely . . . an object for self-gratification."

[74]Northrop Frye, p. 37.

[75]R.M. Frye, p. 59.

[76]Eve's gesture has met with opposing reactions from the critics. B. Rajan, for example, praises the "self-sacrificing majesty" of Eve at this point, which, he says, affirms "Milton's faith in man's goodness" (p. 76). But Roland Frye sees this and her later acts of self-denial as indicative of "the limits of her sinful nature" which are "only more subtle forms of self-centeredness, of anguish and regret" (p. 68). And surely, as Adam realizes, her desire to bear all the punishment is excessive and unwise; she is

> Unwary, and too desirous, as before
> So now of what thou know'st not.   (847-48)

Yet I would argue that we are not to judge Eve too harshly here. Although her offer is unwise, it is at least motivated by unselfish love for Adam and is, thus, a step in the right direction, for she says that she would bear the punishment of death to spare him, which is more than Adam's suicidal disobedience, in which he does not think of sparing her.

[77] Hughes, p. 168.

[78] Lawrence A. Sasek, "The Drama of Paradise Lost, Books XI and XII," in Milton: Modern Essays in Criticism, ed. Arthur E. Barker (New York: Oxford Univ. Press, 1965), p. 347.

[79] Mary Ann Radzinowicz, "'Man as a Probationer of Immortality': Paradise Lost, XI-XII," in Approaches to Paradise Lost: The New York Tercentenary Lecture, ed. C.A. Patrides (Toronto: Univ. of Toronto Press, 1968), p. 39.

[80] From The Temple in The Works of George Herbert, ed. F.E. Hutchinson (Oxford: Clarendon Press, 1941).

[81] Areopagitica, Hughes, pp. 728-29.

Book of Nature, 1, 89-91, 93

Briefe Method of Catechising, A (Egerton), 29, 45

Browne, Sir Thomas, 13, 124

Bruce, Robert, 32-33

Bunyan, John, 51, 125

"Burial of an Infant, The" (Vaughan), 20-21

Burton, Robert, 131, 140, 152 n. 30

Byfield, Nicholas, 4, 12, 29, 43, 47, 58 n. 28, 64

Calling, 46-48, 87-88, 143, 146

Calvin, John, 1, 20, 31, 43, 46, 51

Caritas, 100-01, 117, 120, 125, 138, 141, 144

Catholics, 47, 57 n. 18

Centuries of Meditations (Traherne), 30, 72, 77-81, 83-96, 124-25

Certaine Plaine, briefe, and comfortable Notes, upon every Chapter of Genesis (Babington), 12, 17, 69

Christian Dictionary, A (Wilson), 12

Christian Doctrine (Milton), 122, 124, 128-29, 136, 138-39, 142-43, 146-47, 150 n. 7

Christian Ethicks (Traherne), 33-34, 44, 77, 86-88, 94-95, 100-01, 106, 114, 122, 139-40, 146, 149

Christian heroism, 43, 99, 103, 109-11, 143, 145-59

"City, The" (Traherne), 83

City of God, The (Augustine), 44, 101, 123

Collection of Ancient and Modern Prophesies, A (Lilly), 66-67

Columbus, Christopher, 10

"Com Holy Ghost Eternal God" (Tra-

herne), 87-88

Commentary of John Calvin Upon the first booke of Moses called Genesis, A, 20

Commentary on the . . . Epistle of S. Paul to the Romanes (Wilson), 4, 20

Commentary Upon the First and Second Chapters of St. Paul to the Colossians, A (Bayne), 33

Comus (Milton), 99

Confession, 48-50, 88, 143-44

Confessions (Augustine), 2-3, 33, 48, 51

Contrition, 48-50, 88, 143-44, 146

Conviction, 48-49, 88, 143-44

Crooke, Samuel, 4, 12-13, 29, 44

Cupiditas, 100-01, 117, 138, 141

Dante Alighieri, 10

Davies, John of Hereford, 13

Dent, Arthur, 29, 45

Devine Weekes (Du Bartas), 31

Diatribae (Mede), 66

Diodati, John, 17-18, 43

"Distraction" (Vaughan), 36

Divine Comedy, The (Dante), 10

Divine Herbal (Adams), 3-4

Divine Pymander of Hermes Mercurius Trismegistus, The (Everard), 19

Donne, John, 13, 20, 34, 44, 49, 53-54, 64-65, 70-72, 88

"Dooms-day" (Herbert), 65

Double Catechisme, A (Bernard), 45

Downame, John, 16

Du Bartas, Guillaume de Salluste, 31

159

nesse" (Donne), 44

"I am a Little World Made Cunningly" (Donne), 53-54

Idolatry, 101, 104, 130-31, 137, 140

Ignatian Meditation, 89, 99

In Festo Sancti Michaelis Archangeli
(Austin), 5

Innocence, the State of, 1-2, 4-5,
9-26, 77-84, 91-93, 99, 121-41,
146, 150 n. 6

"Innocence" (Traherne), 79, 91-92

Institution of Christian Religion,
The (Calvin), 1, 31

Isidore of Seville, St., 10-11

Jackson, Thomas, 5, 15, 29, 31, 35,
43, 46, 51, 54-55

Jung, C.G., 80-83

Justifying Faith (Jackson), 54

Key of the Revelation, The (Mede),
68

Lever, Christopher, 16, 29, 47-48

Leviathan (Hobbes), 29

Lilly, William, 66-67

Lok, Henry, 31

"Longing" (Herbert), 48-49

Love, 2, 16, 18, 43, 69, 71-72, 84,
88-90, 93-96, 99-104, 109-111,
114, 116-20, 125-26, 128-32,
134-42, 144, 146-49, 154-55
n. 76

Luther, Martin, 67-68

"Lycidas" (Milton), 110

"Man" (Traherne), 56

Man in Glory (Anselmus), 20, 64,
69-72

Manichees, 10

"Mankind is Sick" (Traherne), 34-35

Mappe of Mans Mortalitie, A
(Moore), 55

Mede, Joseph, 66, 68

Meditation, 4, 30, 37, 77, 87-94

Meditations on the Six Days of Creation (Traherne), 13, 31, 54,
77, 87-88

Microcosmographie (Earle), 21-22,
35-36

Millenium, the, 66-68, 105

Milton, John, 14-15, 17-18, 31, 43-
44, 55, 66-67, 99-149

"Misapprehension" (Traherne), 85-86

Misery, the State of, 1-5, 29-40, 77,
84-86, 99-101, 104-05, 107,
110-11, 113-14, 116, 120, 125-
26, 130-31, 140-42, 146, 149,
150 n. 6, 152 n. 30

Moore, John, 55

More, Henry, 17, 54, 64, 71-72

"Morning-Watch, The" (Vaughan), 52

Mutability, 32-35, 111

"My Spirit" (Traherne), 83

Nature, the State of. See Misery

Neoplatonists, 20

Newe Anatomie of whole man, A
(Woolton), 15-16, 20, 32, 50,
55, 69-70, 72

Of Reformation (Milton), 66-67

Origen, 18

Original sin, 29-30, 33, 35, 79-80,
96-97 n. 5, 142

Paradise. See Eden

Virgil, 9

Wagner, Richard, 139

"When I Consider how my Light is
    Spent" (Milton), 143

Wilson, Thomas, 4, 12, 20

"Wonder" (Traherne), 78, 82

Woolton, John, 15-16, 20, 32, 50,
    55, 69-70, 72

Wordsworth, William, 78

Works and Days (Hesiod), 9

Wyatt, Sir Thomas, 130

Diane Elizabeth Dreher is Associate Professor of English and Director of Interdisciplinary Studies at the University of Santa Clara, California. She received her Ph.D. and M.A. in English from the University of California, Los Angeles, her B.A. in English and Comparative Literature from the University of California, Riverside, and has studied at the Shakespeare Institute at Stratford-Upon-Avon. She has received research grants from the National Endowment for the Humanities, the Andrew Mellon Foundation, and the Danforth Foundation and has consulted on interdisciplinary programs for the National Endowment for the Humanities. The author of numerous articles, reviews and papers on Renaissance and seventeenth-century poetry and drama, Dr. Dreher has recently published an Augustan Reprint Society edition of John Banks's Vertue Betray'd, Or Anna Bullen (1682), the first tragedy in English with an historical woman as sole protagonist.